Frederick Pollack

A Poverty of Words

for T. C. Porter
with thanks for his interest
& for his fine journal Upender —

I hope you enjoy This —

Fred Pollack
DC 3/16/15

A Poverty of Words

Frederick Pollack

ISBN-13: 978-1632750198
ISBN-10: 1632750198
Published by Prolific Press Inc., Harborton, VA.
Edited by: Glenn Lyvers
Cover Painting by: Phylis Geller
Cover Photo by: James Mahoney
Author Photo by: Paul Kaller
Library of Congress Control Number: 2014956929
Printed in the USA.

For Phylis

If you don't do what you believe in,
you end up believing in what you do.

— *Xavier Rubert de Ventos*

Contents...

Foreword

Frederick Pollack's poetry is a national treasure. During my years as editor of Story Line Press, the book I most loved discovering was Pollack's long narrative poem, *The Adventure*. It still thrills me. I was fortunate to publish his book, *Happiness*, and I've been reading this author's poems ever since.

Pollack has a singular dedication to poetry. I know of no living poet who works harder, or who brings such a range of knowledge to his subjects, which are always ambitious and revelatory. Donald Hall once remarked that 'Fred might be the kind of poet who labors in obscurity, then becomes famous after he dies.' I hope not. No one writes like Pollack; his poems are political, philosophical, musical, and culturally savvy. Like his character, Ovid, Pollack is a smart and compassionate stranger in a strange land. He's funny in unexpected ways – "He dreamed of telephones and email,/though they looked like Cupid and gulls" – and always great company.

Pollack is capable of beginning a poem, as he does "Petting Zoo," with a line as odd as "You can't hold adult/koalas." Then he shows why and arrives at the off-kilter but perfectly apt question: "Doesn't quite fit the image?" This is a great secret of his verse: he is always pushing the envelope of the image to find the after-image of the thing itself. In "Drink to That," he describes a man in a bar as "a mouth pursued by the sharpest sweetness/or memory of pain./You know this is the wrong eternity;/the knowledge guarantees you will remain." The poet's task is to stand fearlessly in the truth of that observation. It's never the place one wants to be, but we don't choose our battlefield.

If you've never read this poet, prepare for one of the great breakthroughs of your reading life.

— Robert McDowell, author of *Poetry as Spiritual Practice*, *The World Next to This One*, *On Foot*, *In Flames*; editor emeritus and director, Story Line Press.

Diotima

Regrettably she has no sponsor
in our world, and when she applies
for a visa, it's denied –
bureaucratic fingers
balk at "Purpose of Visit."
(How thick the walls of our embassy,
its windows narrow, blank, and barred.)
Then Diotima shrugs,
turns. Beret, trenchcoat,
perfume again pass
our guard (it is her imperturbability
he loathes), re-cross the boulevard,
reclaim her table on that street of tables.
There, unbothered –
nobody tries to *pick up* Wisdom
though all desire her – she takes out
her notebook, reflects.
With Plato she was an enabler.
For Hölderlin, a joy just out of reach.
What might she have whispered
to me, if Immigration had let her through?
She fills a page, removes and crumples it.
At the edges of the street,
fast-food joints have begun to replace
the cafés, but for the moment
it's four o'clock; trumpets sound from the castle;
a carriage brings a smiling and waving archduke.

Heartland

When, for the fourth time that summer,
the sky blackens, and wind
shoves and pulls and howls in
all directions, but this time closer,
seriously, here –
someone, perhaps Dad, remembers
the business about getting into a bathtub;
and they all get into the bathtub
and hug, with the littlest
shrieking among knees. Mom
would kill, even now, for a drink;
the boy is catatonic, the girl
loudly, inaudibly sings.
But now, no one remembers Dad's
somewhat pro forma beatings,
fights, inexorable cheating,
or his or her own variously inflicted
scars. And as the wind removes
parts of the roof, siding, drywall,
stuff, the rest of the roof, the shower-curtain
wraps somehow around them
as if to join and bless
their hug. When they step
from the tub and climb
over boards and scraps into
a flawless evening, they are still,
wonderfully, "we";
and need not for the moment ask
why God etc., hear moaning neighbors,
or doubt that someone will help them
rebuild, in the same way, in the same place.

Hello Again

The Buddha, reconstituted
in a distant future, disappoints:
one hopes for detached, ironic, timeless
reason but his mind is full
of augurs, gods, and the several "Baskets"
of his system. Still, he's flexible –
more so than any number
of later theorists he meets
in the dining hall and rec room or
floating in brain-gel over the grounds.
He learns without interest
the history since his time,
inquires why we revived him, seems
politely annoyed at our response.
One afternoon he asks
for death. Asked why,
he says, "To ascend." When told
it's no longer an option, he appears
more amused than anything, somehow
pitying. Eventually released,
though promising to check in, he makes
a "pilgrimage" through formerly
religious former deserts
to an ancient cliff that once contained
huge images of him and now the void.

Aunt

As time passed and her date
didn't appear, she had another drink
and smoked another cigarette.
Subtly, without seeming to,
her wide-brimmed hat
blocked every line of sight
from other tables to her face,
which nonetheless aged.
For an hour she imitated
a statue called "Serenity,"
"Reflection" perhaps,
or even "Freedom,"
then ordered a dinner
she could never afford.

The waiter lit her cigarettes
with an astonishingly
calibrated balance
between invisibility
and grace. When the time came,
he displayed the wine list
but left her psychic room
to choose a cheap red. Somehow
ran interference
between the impatient
maître d' and her; absorbed,
deflected what might otherwise have been
stares. But this charity
was no part of her story.

As time passed, cellphones
insured that reasons
would be made instantly clear, that no one
could be abandoned. Smoking
was banned, so that the lives of diners
were long and fulfilled. Recorded music
lifted moods. And a new
democratic openness
prevailed. If she had waited,
the waiter would

have introduced himself, said *I'll be your savior*
tonight, thrown off
his tux, her late bad marriage,
and taken into his her bony hand.

Guardi

Something is always *wrong*. The walls
have the same greasy gleam
as the distant, averted faces.
The path under half an arch
beside effaced obelisks
leads nowhere, is walked
by a one-legged beggar, perhaps
an old soldier, viewed by a beggar.
Water is some other fluid,
which the della Salute and the palazzi
drink and sweat.
When oil burns
at San Marcuola, in the year,
coincidentally, of the Bastille,
the rear-view crowd is vivid and inert.
A mattress in the window
of a house halfway to nothing airs
only its bugs.

       He was always, no doubt,
respectful, i.e.,
behaving, without status, like a courtier,
however patently inferior
the patron: rackrenting minor
gentry, poxy bishop, or
the Doge's lackey with his countless airs.
Perhaps he laughed about them with his family
firm; then, brooding
between drawings as seasick light
crossed his mildewed ceiling, felt
that boredom only known
to ages of transition.
Realizing at some point
that the ruins so attractive
to him and everyone, stuck in everywhere
in painting, faked
by nobles, were not Rome's,
or even Venice's or his, but *ours*;
the secret gave him reason to go on.

After the Rehearsal

I wanted to celebrate The Dance ... but the woman
in charge (choreographer? director?)
asked how I could, and why she should let me,
me with no experience of dance,
not even the terms, and broken down
enough to be disturbing here –
at best a dirty old man, at worst
a *memento mori*? Truthfully
she asked not in words
but with the stance of her body,
as old as mine but vastly
more limber: a squint
of the hips, one mournful shoulder. While
her dancers, having rehearsed for hours,
stood but were never still – flexing
eyebrows and thighs, impassive,
perfect in tights and leotards
(though the room smelled like a stable).
Heartbroken, I moaned how
the phrase The Dance had always
annoyed me, sloppy metaphor
for everything, sex and life.
But with the least shift
of their weight, the corps and their chief
accused me of a lack
not only of vitality but vital focus!
So I left, staggered out. Or no,
not staggering – placing
my left foot to the left,
right to the right, bridging
the gap with my cane,
eventually my walker ... Outside,
the clouds of that sunset
remained themselves, rooted,
only their colors moving,
colors of love and ash and glaciers.

Nearer to Thee

He has already dressed himself:
tie perfect, zipper not,
a scrap of toilet paper at his heel.
Submitting as we fuss and praise,
he silently endures our casual clothes
that prove us neither grown nor serious.
Soon, in a residence, among
smells mustier, stains hardier than his suit's,

there will, he knows, be no more trips
except to clinics and a funeral;
and so he wheezes dismissive thanks
and makes obligatory eye-contact.
Accepting help through drifts of bills
long paid – a sort of proof –
he pauses at the threshold of the light
and settles, hieratic, in the car.

The ten miles of the drive before
the important drive provide
no stimulation, nothing meaningful.
Retail, which, if it failed, deserved
to fail, or which deserves its crowds,
and whose ads he absorbs
in much the way he listens to us
spinning our lives for him in keen detail.

He used to pretend, arriving where
we're going, it was the vaulted
flowering boughs over winding lanes,
the massed forsythia and tulip beds
he liked. But it was always
the houses, separate enough
to feel imperial yet perceive allies,
coy behind trees but wonderfully there.

The houses – not the bodies at their pools
or alfresco, sometimes glimpsed beyond
the crests of sculpted hills. For those
were rotting, though well-tended,

or youthful and commensurately funded,
and pained him either way. Perhaps
he roamed wine-cellars, studies, bedrooms,
richer because unseen; it's hard to say.

The houses, old made new then new
forever; full of good
or questionable things – which doesn't matter.
What counts is ease of being, the grace
their owners have in owning: half
in vulgar time where anyone can see them,
half on a sort of screen
whose glow still fills and dims his ancient eyes.

And now this neighborhood, quaint term, may be
the last of its type without walls or guards.
As we take him back
through condos, malls, and rot, he seems
almost to seek our faces, now
no doubt as vacant as his own, and to want
to apologize, though not
to us particularly, for some lack.

Trickle-down

Only the rich and powerful
are real. Not the "famous";
fame is prolefeed.
Any punk who shoots up his school,
a congressional Democrat or other punks,
has it. Even the sexiest
Hollywood star stands
where he or she is told, says the words,
rinses, repeats – i.e., acts
like anyone merely paid.
But wealth and power lie beyond
the obedient world;
are the neoplatonic One
that emanates, progressively debased,
towards it.
Turbulence over crusted mac
and cheese in some doublewide
palely imitates negotiations
with or for a leverage-wife
that start on the Grounds and are taken inside.
Likewise with thought, disdained by those who know.
When Charles or David stiffs a doorman –
never tipping, however much he bears
to the limo – it isn't because
they despise him for being there
but because he thinks they are.

Lesson

There are two choices: guard,
con. And protocols,
easy to follow, for each.
It's intolerable, therefore,
when a guard talks
with cons, disregarding
rules and guard wisdom. When he
defends weaker from stronger
cons, and from guards. When,
however politely, he doubts
the protocols of strength.

Such a guard finds, i.e., loses
himself at last confronting
that agent
for whom pretense is substance, want is wealth,
tattoos the living flesh;
who knees him down and shows the knife
and represents the law.

Tristia

1

When Ovid, arriving in exile,
was met by the centurion and prefect
of the settlement, their attitude towards him
was already largely decided.
He was of high rank,
had been popular; the grounds
of the Emperor's quarrel with him
were classified; no order had come
for an unfortunate incident or accident.
More importantly, he still
had money. If Augustus
forgave and recalled him
they'd hold a big dinner,
have him read
his works, give him a wreath, and maybe
he'd put in a good word
back home. So they regarded him
the way one regards
someone of one's own class
who is just over the narrow shifting line
of luck: i.e., as human. And Ovid
raised his eyes to take in
their faces, wondered if charm
were required, decided it wasn't,
and – whether because he was applying
no imagination, or because imagination
hadn't reached this point yet –
found in them no comparison
to the harsh seas and rocks,
the terrors he had traversed; they were merely
dull. They saw him
to his quarters, mildewed and small but sound enough,
and arranged for provisions and slaves.

2

He missed his wife. News
of her failed attempts
to speak with Augustus, his secretary,
undersecretaries, Senators,
of the clear refusal
to allow her to join him, of her
having finally to sell
the house in town, of her health,
took sometimes a year
to arrive. He dreamed of telephones and email,
though they looked like Cupid and gulls.
Surely, if he could only *talk*
to Augustus, he could clear things right up;
and if he could talk to her
he could tell her what to say,
and if he could talk to her ...
no, he would not feel less alone.
Time passing without knowledge
reduced the number of things
in time. Some, like his original "crime"
(such as it was), and Augustus,
and friends who didn't write,
were large decaying ruins
like Pyramids. But his wife
was a building somehow newer and
more whole for the vines
growing round it ... He was alarmed
how much he loved her.
It seemed un-Roman. In letters
and epistolary poems he worked
ceaselessly to return to Rome, where poets
had mistresses and boys and played
at love and being destroyed by love.

3

When the loose tribes of nomads
generically called Scythians
were becalmed or distant, he could walk outside
the walls. He walked by the sea,
not as we do, to fade into
the infinite, only to walk.
The sea was evil, the cliffs and the immense
sky the colors of exile.
Smelly barbarian traders in rabbit-fur
pants, without meaningful language,
horrified him when
they crossed his path in town.
Once, perhaps, he sat on a slope,
looking so miserable
that a Scythian girl gave him
milk fresh from her mare. (As Delacroix
repeatedly imagined, the Scythians
rotating somehow around Ovid,
not quite ignoring or ignored.)
– Unlikely; no truer than Rome
the day of his exile being
the golden ecstasy
Turner painted. As he walked, he saw
these images people would make of him,
believed he was losing his mind,
and repressed them. Thinking
how, as a citizen,
he was sworn to defend
the town if the barbarians attacked:
nearsightedly aiming
an arrow, limply raising
a sword beneath the cold eye of the prefect.

4

Tiberius, the dour reclusive sadist
who succeeded Augustus, saw no
need to rescind Ovid's exile,
and gradually the poet died.
Shutters and oiled hides
kept out, more or less, the damp.
His last slave tended the fire.
Sometimes, asleep, he took
her bony, crusted hand in his
and it felt soft and familiar.
He ignored the last letters.
There was no attack; the nomads migrated elsewhere.
Waking, he had more of those visions
of future things, which he now recognized
as such, but without interest;
they all seemed cruel, overblown,
fads of the rabble, merely *new* –
not, as they should be, mutations
of former things, the work of gods and magic.
(He liked, however, the statue
the Romanians built in the harbor
of their seedy port; it didn't resemble him
in the least, but noble brooding
was a look he could have worn
if called upon.)
At the end, scraped down to a tone,
he considered metamorphosis,
his great insight and principle,
doubtful.

The Moving Walkway Is Ending
-Reagan National

You'll have enough time
to distinguish (suddenly) irony
that supports disaffection, critique, revolution
and attacks the powers-that-be
from the reverse,
and to shift your suitcase
for someone passing (on the left),
and to worry, faintly,
which type yours is,
and to scratch, covertly,
a familiar inaccessible itch
(travel-nerves). Ahead, in the concourse,
fellow passengers
(here more than elsewhere "fellow"-nothing,
a they) move slowly,
peer for their gates,
gaze at the Capitol, seem to
pose by displays of high-end watches
and Ray-bans. You pass Jacklin's mural,
The Skaters,
fuzzy silhouetted sprites
in a light rather like that
now filling the concourse, a triumphal twilight.
The other art is abstract. Reagan
would have approved, i.e., not noticed,
though it's unlike
the helmeted generic football player
he liked to doodle in margins
of summaries of summaries. Your flight is delayed.
The security line fills the concourse.
Mentally you prepare yourself
to remove your shoes, belt, wallet, watch, and keys.
Mentally you worry
how long you can insert
compressed philosophical allusions, like tubes
of gel, into your work in place of symbols.
Since Tyner's valiant cry, "Don't touch my junk!",
they have been using "blob"
instead of "naked" imaging in walk-throughs.
It occurs to you that when you used to

imagine a future it involved laughter –
extreme, histrionic
laughter perhaps – but no irony.

Moonrise

1

We met over the years,
but never in one room at the same time.
When someone was successful, envy
made the others talk for hours
with insincere, hence forgettable brilliance.
Time gnawed off parts of us,
and often we discussed
what honors they were accumulating
(like Gogol's "Nose"), what parties dazzling
(like the Emperor Hadrian's little soul)
without us.
(As if late sexuality, hot as ever,
vain and buffed as never before
after an antimatter spa,
now in motels beyond the cosmos
were showing how it's done ...)
Meanwhile we wasted or hoarded love.
Somebody's child brought in
a toy, a "Transformer," and we marveled
how a car becomes a plane, which becomes
a man, at every stage eager for battle.
An adolescent (possibly the same
creature), whom a parent introduced
to us in passing, seemed remarkably polite;
at least we remarked it, knowing
he saw us as barely human.
Wives talked, husbands talked, and came
to the end of evenings,
as I to the end of thirty lines,
having perceived nothing.
It's the system, one cried, that trivializes
and drains us. Age, cried another.
Each is an arm of the other,
said someone else – which could have been important,
so we denied it to each other,
made it our own, and marked it to consider
later. If in all these years
there had been one point, like a faith but not really,

a fact, a spark where we touched ...
(Thus the most wistful, who could not move on.)
Another shook his head: But isn't it
process that matters, a certain open-
endedness of meaning? No, I said.

2

We wandered onto the veranda,
mildly surprised there was one,
and that city had given way
to a breeze as crisp as a logical proof
and a sky with stars.
We had always expected, it seemed,
someday to be translated, *aufgehoben* –
we rational ones who had had to smile
self-deprecatingly at reason,
we the haplessly cultured – and now had been.
A full moon rose, very near, and we saw
the great tracks bringing
molybdenum and tungsten from Mare Imbrium
to the base at Ptolemaeus,
the lights that marked the water mines
near the poles, the other domes
and excavations at Tycho.
That is, I delighted in naming these things
with the callow metallic cheer
of a techie; and my friends delighted
in mourning, protesting
the theft of nature, the omnipresent spoor
of man or the system. Thus we improvised
roles we immediately felt to be
cliché. Then the moon rebooted,
rising again in fragments like
a tacky-sublime effect
in an aging remake of *The Time Machine*,
jagged and looming.
We cried out. Our environment
seemed blighted, as if never to leave
the thick night, and as passive as ourselves.
Then the moon illuminated it
one last time, and this time
was arty. A larger version of that form

Brancusi played with
in *Mademoiselle Pogany*
and in his *Sleeping Muse*. Then it opened its eyes.

The Recession

The suits seem under a curse
that keeps them in the sun.
They stand, not sit, by a table
too frail to support
their mumbled part in the great Deal,
which thrives however markets go.
Sometimes they glance at the pool
and share in the joint venture of a leer.
On a deck-chair, a young hero
taps his iPad, which also
sings to him through earbuds,
while on his thigh another phone
vibrates; there's no way
failure could penetrate
that phalanx. But he has no time for nymphs.
Nearby, a serial divorcee
settles like ancient mountains.
She too, behind vast sunglasses,
looks at the water,
then at the parking-lot, three-quarters empty,
and the guests who arrived this morning:
a couple near the deep end,
urgently talking without smiles or charm.

The two girls in the pool race,
then bob just beyond
where their long legs could stand,
then float in the shallows and laugh in tones like wine.
They are not twenty-somethings,
but precisely whatever age
they are. And what? Not students.
Not owned, by debt or wealth.
How are they possible?
Let alone those bodies in their nothing suits.
You could die for the blonde, kill for the redhead,
but more for the expression
they have as they climb up and out
and look back, briefly. A single drop
falls from a breast towards the concrete,
vanishing before it lands.

Further Adventures

When Rabbi Löwy struck
the Aleph from among
the letters on the Golem's brow, changing
EMET ("eternal") to MET ("death"),
the creature toppled, and was carried
to an empty room atop
the synagogue. On the street,
people the thing had killed,
Gentiles and Jews, were also taken away
and survivors stared at the Rabbi.
"Our beloved Emperor," he said,
"has rescinded his edict
against the Jews of Prague.
The abomination fulfilled
its purpose. But at such cost!
I should have known it would be
unmanageable, unable
to tell friend from foe, or foe from neutral,
its clay hand raised against all others.
When rain has removed this blood,
I shall be left with guilt
and you with a myth,
ambiguous like any myth,
and as small compared to the Law."
Perhaps because of these words,
though in every pogrom
of the following centuries Jews
looked to that window
which may have marked its room,
the Golem never reappeared.
It's said that an SS lieutenant
took a knife to stab it
and was never seen again, but that story
may be apocryphal.
Over time, even the moisture
recalling spirit in the Golem's clay
dried, and the creature
became friable, smaller.
Yet a strange potency remained.
It may have been the talk of freedom

that stirred it in '89,
although several more years
passed in a sort of pain.
Until, in a new hotel
as streamlined as a submarine,
full of fresh-faced, madly ambitious
and incompetent staff, a woman
from the IMF lost it, shrieking, "What do you *mean*
you can't get a connection to
New York? I have been waiting
TWO HOURS.
I can't do business under these conditions!"
Then suddenly her scream
changed as she saw,
on a street still called Leninova,
the Golem halting new BMWs,
and the last Tatras and Skodas, visibly
flaking like itself. How had it crossed
town? In darkness probably,
beside walls its own color. But now
it had stopped
in the sun. It was confused
by the sun, and a lack of instructions,
but also by the beings, people,
staring. The terrible need to do battle
remained, but what it saw
was neither friends nor enemies nor neutrals,
only things like itself, warring mud,
with neither "death" nor "deathless" on their brows.
So without a word (it had no mouth),
the Golem ran into a wall
that had belonged to the secret police
and would soon house a Swiss bank,
forming a somewhat turtle-shaped
bulge in the stucco. It isn't
part of the normal Prague tour,
or touted in guidebooks beside
the craze for monster trucks and Kafkaburgers.

The Kid

No one recalled how the Kid joined the gang.
Was he found freezing
in the doorway of their bar?
Or stealing pizza from someone's floor

while everyone slept? He began, no doubt,
with a beating, but the boss
(who was called Big Man) felt a sort
of fondness. Don't you have

a Mama or Grandmamma? he asked.
But the Kid apparently didn't.
He answered every question
but always with a whine

that annoyed the others. But Big Man
said Let him be. Which didn't stop them
or make him stop them
from playing cruel jokes, and making

an occasional quasi-bitch
of the Kid. To all of which
he responded impassively, which counted,
they decided, as courage. Some fool

once mentioned school. Everyone laughed.
Big Man said I'll teach him
whatever he needs. So the Kid
stood lookout and ran

deliveries, competently, and
eventually pulled a trigger,
but missed
and mumbled and whined

when he had to do that. Years
passed. Big Man noticed
that the Kid didn't grow.
Which he thought was funny, and drew

a mustache on him, made him shave
nothing off, had
the others rub him
against some serious or laughing bitch

to no effect. A day came
when Big Man lay in bed
with tubes in his arms and cops
at the door, and because

of the cops or being dead,
no visitors. Except the Kid.
Strange child, said the boss (more or less),
was it you who betrayed me? And the Kid

said No, but it doesn't matter.
With illusion departing
you may be prepared to learn
there is only humiliation and pain.

Embrace the former to lose the latter.

Wait For It

Rodents inherit, evolve, and
after many ages form
an image of us. But they are mild and communal
and think we were merely solitary and cruel.
They envy our power –
how could they not? There are so many
poisoned places, still –
and the sky remains so heavy
they seldom see the stars
they know they will never reach.
The sun will swell, the sea will boil.
It isn't, however, science
but religion that tells them so,
as well as that the next life
endlessly edits this.

Minor Oracle

The big dog seeks the small lap.
The merchant is dressed like the king.
Lovers, having enjoyed
great sex, do not use the phrase
until later. Wisdom, painfully
gathered, is readily forgotten.
The dishwasher that cleans
well enough but smells musty
when opened remains in use.
The viewpoints of distant planets
are valid. Laughter drains
with water. The black sun yearns to implode.

More than Generous

One of our beloved billionaires
must be behind it, must have signed
the foundation behind it into being.
One of those men whose well-known features
remain somehow forever indistinct.
He tours the rooms of the upper floors,
the common room, the kitchen;
randomly touches drapes and fixtures;
appears unfocused. But his aides are paid,
as he says, to be tunnel-visioned,
and drag him out, and load him into his limo.
Guests start to arrive.
The first are what you'd expect:
the passive, needy, and rejected:
graying ponytails, polite abstracted tenors,
eyes fixed on imagined scenes
of compensatory violence
as if upon a missed receding train.
Yet those who, elsewhere, command
or at least shout, and are adored
or boast they are, appear also;
and though at first they straighten ties and glare,
they find themselves, or perhaps you find them,
crouching in hallways like
the other sort, whose weakness here is strength.
They peer around corners for enemies
but there are no enemies here.
Someone who could be, who is elsewhere empowered
by vicious faith, enters and strides
directly to a window, and looks out
on streets that might as well be walls,
and remains there.
Towards evening, women claim the common room.
They are generally older,
and know the light is unflattering,
but are past caring, though not perhaps past
the hope of a word. But people sleep alone here
and seldom exactly talk. For when two
approach each other, one recedes infinitely,
or swells and swells till, of two seekers, one

is crushed, the other bursts.
Only in deep night, which could be day
elsewhere, the billionaire –
he may be dreaming elsewhere but not here –
roams, like a devoted concierge,
the corridors and stairwells, scattering
on everyone a sort of dandruff.
It may be this that keeps them coming back
or staying, often for many years,
often till death. Upon which
the guests incuriously hobble forth,
bearing a friend through the surrounding dust.

Night Building

Though it slows you at dusk on the highway,
you like, when you reach it, that intense
oval of light where workers
(though they always look stopped or half-stopped)
efficiently bury
pipes, resurface, or aim
an offramp at some subdivided void.
They're sublime, those lights; the crew
can only look down or ahead;
and lights, machines, and workers
intimidate yet reassure.
Later, away from your vehicle, construction
persists but is only a matter
of sound – gears seeking
and rejecting each other, engines
balking, wheezing black
into black, matter being chewed
and spread. And a sense, not so much
of danger or the anger
of busy men, but constraint, an absolute
need to stay this side
of the orange lattices, the yellow tape. But which is
this side? You can't see
the tape, dare not feel for
the Jersey barriers, basically
can't move; because mud, the void, the teeth
of bulldozers, I-beams swinging from a crane
may be anywhere. In summer you clutch
the sheet, in winter the duvet, in
that heat or cold to which they, the
workers, seem indifferent. How do they see
in this gloom? And what are they building? You
had thought post-industrial
capitalism was somehow less
material. It's as if the branching highway
had fused with the malls and the pre-frayed
apartments it was to have served. You try
to ask, diffidently, one
of the shapes moving invisibly past,
then think better of it,

or worse; ask whether
construction will extend
indefinitely into the space
where dawn was.

Is This a Dagger

Sleepless, a king walks
his smoky torchlit halls.
May pause at any door,
nod at snores,
frown at words and sighs
beyond, dither at silence,
lose himself in a mere
vertical drowse.
Could enter and demand
company, expect
obsequiousness, disloyalty.
Won't; the only traitor
is his body.
Elsewhere, peasants grunt
at dreams, sentries stare
into fire, prisoners
dissolve chains with tears.
All give what they can.
If only sleep or dawn
would come, or (he remembers)
Christ, alternative to both.
If only a foolish
sword would appear
at the end of the hall! But the guards,
armored and visored
at the ends of the hall, are his,
gleam and are still.
If I looked, would I find (he wonders)
an eye within the steel?

RSVP

When all the friends of your youth, dead or otherwise,
have entered a zone
inaccessible to cell-phone,
Google, email, social media
and private detection, you're free
without occultist hype to summon them
for dinner or drinks. Don't worry
if few or any were ever
in the same room together –
wasn't that true of so many
illustrious *cénacles*? You imagine,
tremulously, the talk,
the affair picking up
exactly where it ended. And wisdom bestowed –
as if those speaking eyebrows,
that sneer you always tacitly obeyed,
kept watch over decades
and now may explain and forgive.
But when they gather, each face, each body
(apart from the fact they would be
as grey and ill as yours)
appears uneasy.
Your reminiscence of the dorm
or lost *bohème* evokes a smile
through thinner lips than you recall.
Nothing pertinent and some obnoxious
things are said politically.
Boredom prevailed, prevails, and worst of all
there was and is no interest
in you. Perhaps under clotted mascara
or spotted pate, an eye
looks through you at an esoteric sunset.
You tell the worst jokes
and war-stories you've accumulated,
trying for a formerly stylish note of *néant*.
But the party breaks up early, ghosts filter out –
some, it occurs to you,
to gated communities, choice waterfront
acreage before the final home.

The Guard Dies

By droshky, trap, and landau,
the worthy and responsible of the realm
arrive one icy night
at an auxiliary palace deep in the country.
Their horses, glad of rest,
shiver, piteously snort, and are quickly stabled.
Alighting, the Ministers of War,
the Exchequer, Public Order, Education,
and other medaled chests mightier still,
warm in their furs, discuss –
somber, but careless of being heard –
issues of state. The smoke
of pipes and cigars rewards
the single guard, a conscript, young and hale,
whose uniform is gorgeous but too thin,
whom only the officers acknowledge, and
who trembles now with awe as well as cold.

They pass into the palace,
fling off their coats, dine and refresh themselves,
then gather in a glassed and darkened alcove
from which, unseen, unheard, they watch the guard.
During the night older nobles
doze, are laughed awake, and hurry
as they can to the window.
A table groans with dainties, brandy, humidors.
"He's Twentieth Regiment, isn't he?"
asks a civilian, showing off.
"They choose the best." A field marshal
names the boy's province, which is praised.
No bets are laid; it would mean social death
to suggest one. At midnight
the watch should change but doesn't;
and the guard, pale in torchlight,
looks around – the watchers hold their breath –
takes a few steps, slaps his arms,
then comes again to attention.
At one, the constant wind brings heavy snow,
which, to the witnesses' delight, persists.
At three fifteen he slumps, at four

he falls and is swiftly covered;
so that the usual debate occurs,
idle and slurred, whether to wake
and shoot what limbs are left or let him sleep.

Bitch

Later she couldn't recall
what page she was reading
aloud in the gray, torn,
'70s textbook and what
about: wars, laws,
art; or exactly when
a hall nomad
opened the door, looked in,
laughed, looked at her,
said "*Bee*-atch," left and was stopped
by a hallway cop,
cried "Get yo hands off me, fuck,"
and hit the cop so that
he would be taken to jail
and earn respect.
She remembered hearing the fight;
the class heard. A sleeper
woke, loudly
identified and praised
the fighter. A girl
called him the biggest fool. The teacher
made her usual request, then
command. A peripatetic
left the room entirely. A quiet girl
with lice, a small
bedwetting boy
compressed themselves. The teacher
invented a question about
the reading. The girlfriend
of the roused sleeper threatened
the girl who had spoken
without respect. They kicked aside
already broken chairdesks
to reach each other. The teacher
didn't stop them. Eventually
they noticed her
sitting. She was thinking
of her parents' basement.
In the silence she said, "You're victims,
so can't be blamed. Unfortunately

no one else can be,
either. So talking to you,
people always look
a little above your head,
and just let in
the vague impression
of a victim. Whom one forgives.
And you sense this anyway, and don't like it,
because it lacks respect.
But it's difficult to stop."
She had their attention,
and tears from a few frightened
or devoted, heartbreaking ones. And wondered
whether to wait
for three o'clock or leave now,
amazing the hall nomads.

Return to Telegraph

Half a block burned, but the storefronts
seem braced and painted and bear
some stirring official notice.
Places that sell African, Tibetan,
or otherwise mystical trinkets
can remain colorful and mystical,
broke. No one has bought
the chain-linked bookstore. The mural
about the Sixties has been somewhat
cleansed of graffiti. The roof
remains where an onlooker
to a demonstration was shot.
One crazed fortyish boy
with the traditional half-dead dog
hawks art from the pavement,
while in People's Park the homeless,
widely separated, sleep
as if trying to become burial mounds.

There is no sidewalk that does not wear
an ectoplasm of choices or,
more often, accumulations
of time that tip over
into grief, a horror of mirrors,
or resolve – if only the petty,
desperate decision to leave.
In my case, eighteen years,
the last of them now thirty years ago.
At the same table in the Café Med,
someone I used to know
finishes an article
inevitably concerning loneliness, menace,
and what could be accomplished but won't;
makes a few notes, walks out
amidst a passive crowd
of students heading towards campus
and ghosts without power to haunt.

Battle on the Ice

The knights advance on the frozen lake.
The comic effect when they lose their footing
fades as they regain it.
Their flags are soigné spears,
their spears the flags of an abstraction.
They rely on the inhuman
impression they make
of nearly eyeless steel-creatures, tube-men,
to scare us. It works.

It's fear, perhaps, not courage
that roots us, comparatively runty,
in rags, to our end of the lake.
We neither bang on our shields
nor mock. Somewhere inside
we're elsewhere, blind and fond
as puppies, communal as puppies
or our small, patient horses,
yearning for peace –

representing, in short, other values
than the knights who, as our cunning
succeeds, fall in.

Sand

1

Despite its dislike for everything
not itself, the sand
likes trees. When they die
it buffs them
into a sort of stone, then attacks
the stone, till between
a night and a morning, they're gone.
It also has no particular
quarrel with lizards that raise, first
their legs on one side, then the other's,
from it; or snakes and fleas,
or humbler mammals; though no one could say
it supports them. When it reaches
the sea, dismissing
the green of coasts, it contemplates
no rival but an arriviste, and sees
(for all time is one
to sand) brackish shallows,
salt. It likes air,
though it could and will do
without it – likes
to rise with its help, rap playfully
on tanks, men walking, the remaining structures.

2

You might think the women compactly
hunched on cracked mud, wearing
wild dulled colors, with almost
their last portable property
in noses and ears, hair piously
and/or sensibly shrouded, are looking
beyond the wire at the
sand through a filter
of apprehension – the militias
might not be satisfied
this time with the last sacks
of rice and bottles of water

from the UN; or through layers
of ignorance, superstitious
mistrust of the camera, etc.; but
they see it well enough.

To the Bare Walls

Tasteful apocalypses can't prepare one
for the real thing, so why bother?
– An outlet of the Cthulhu cult.
A picture of Himself over the counter:
dinosaur-green and -brown, octopus head,
dragon wings, thug build, but these are just
"the spirit of the thing," Lovecraft said;
all believers know
is that at cycle's end the Lord
of All Things will return to eat us –
that part is the real spirit of the thing.
The temp behind the counter isn't
a member. Isn't paid
to believe, or at all these days.
Keeps phoning his girlfriend, there's no ring;
his concern, though mostly for himself,
approaches love. If customers
came in, he'd be able, barely,
to read from a little card: *We can't say*
He wishes us ill – His motives are totally
unknown – but the result is the same.
With rehearsed pauses and
looks, so that someone who
came in would have an impression,
his last, of thought. The temp is tempted
to leave, despite the mayhem
on the streets – rescue his girl, prove himself
a survivor or get eaten –
but he needs the job. Though the store
is a wreck: only the icon, out of reach,
and on the shelves a few snowglobes.

Paradox of the Actor

It isn't only the mask –
the many, the murderous schedule of,
masks. It's that when not
being fate-crazed, king,
seducer, intellectual, he watches
a game, chats forgettably,
reviews his accounts. And she,
no longer a gymnast or
mountaineer of emotions, tends,
humming, the sturdy sooty
plants on her terrace.

And that's the appeal – that feeling,
destiny, even
the worst, the most boring, ours,
will be removed like makeup.
One stays in character awhile,
through the curtain calls, but then it's
off to the Islands, the long white beach,
the poolside drink beneath stars and thatch
with vaguely familiar people.

The Soundwall

The bisected neighborhood
lives the way a poplar, half cut down,
extrudes barkless boughs and giant
leaves that fall in any wind.

Green, blue, and grey
missions, their sidewalks vacant
at noon, look bruised
where graffiti has been removed.

Few homeless beg
on the boulevard; they station
themselves on the ramp to
the new Home Depot.

(Suburbanites who come for plants
or boards or drills walk to and fro
in the vast aisles with the same
focus as at a gun show.)

Then a street just past
the parking lot ends at the soundwall
of the highway. Which produces
something, not quiet.

Gone asphalt,
four long-unpainted wooden
buildings, a woman
pushing a stroller and leading a little girl

towards one. The woman
walks oddly; the girl
holding her hand is wearing a bright
pink parka.

Now This

In the near future, refugees
from water shortages stare
through wire. Charities
and NGOs, out of water, food,
medicine, money and hope are no longer
out there with them. The stare
goes blind after screaming, clawing,
pointless activity, weird shakes,
and three days.

                CNN, whatever,
never show this part. At most,
the first wars in history
fought without lies, for motives known to all.
Still, media create some comforting
distance: the drowned towers
are picturesque, dikes heroic,
desalination plants
imposing though expensive.
And there are still ads.

I too attempt comfort,
specifying "the future." Also, you'll notice
how I've set my (our)
p.o.v. on which side of the wire?

Waiting for Romney

-October, 2012

Colorless, mostly, from five months' drought,
leaves fall like fish scales.
The local air has managed a nice coolness
though the seas are hot.
None of my familiars –
the drugged and addled poor, the increasingly frantic
petit-bourgeoisie (hostile to all
but its betters), the exemplary victims
who sit beside First Ladies
at State of the Union addresses –
show up; they have gone someplace real,
perhaps have become real, leaving
real beercans in the imaginary garden.

Tubercular hostas and fraying ferns
resist the pathetic fallacy.
A sweet three-legged dog hops over,
wanting love.
My neighbor can't afford him and has no friends –
what will he choose? What will the dog choose?
A presence looms in the mild day,
well-meaning, brutal when crossed, to answer
the hope for redemptive violence
in all life. Even the deer,
who come at twilight if they survive
the street. They are as beautiful as religion;
one needn't think how they thirst.

The Origins of Mystery

Beset in childhood by peers,
a certain type of person turns
away from faces joyfully fulfilling
themselves through mockery and spit and
repeated unanswerable questions.
And the one who turns away
attempts a certain smile,
no longer intended to avert
pain (it can only invite it),
but to suggest that beyond
faces and fists the one beset
perceives another world. He had no idea,
previously, of that world;
has none now, except that
it's empty of peers; but it exists
because the smile requires it,
because he has sacrificed
the rest of childhood to it.
And the ones around him
are stone he will walk through
(shattering them in the process)
to reach it, while he
is stone on which they will shatter.

Such are the origins of mystery,
which is everywhere and inevitably
subject to hysterical
distortions: that it's accessible
to anyone; that it is generous,
an open prospect, not suffused
with blood; that it has content.

Straight On Till Morning

Kids looking at something
at the base of a tree. Not an elf,
weirder; golden mantis perhaps;
magic flower, or just a flower.

The mantis is explaining
secrets of adulthood even
adults don't know, and joking. –
Not a flower: a big fungus,

a bug that wants them to go away.
The surrounding yard
lacks lumpen flotsam,
is clearly upper-middle-class;

if you wish, endless.
What happens is they
don't kick the mushroom, squash the bug.
Some concatenation

of artful repression,
drugs, sublimation
annuls the urge. So that
they turn, cross the grass,

their big heads now
forever out of proportion
to their bodies, their eyes mild.
A casual

gesture on their part
draws from the distance
cries, as of someone
forbidden to torture.

Bleb

He doesn't have to *do* much:
look in, with ritual
casualness, at one muddy hovel,
then cross, attended,
the mud to the next. Women
would lie in the mud
to protect his feet; he gestures
them up, they love that.
In one hut someone is sick; he touches
her; they cry and shout.
Or she dies and they cry for his prayer, exult
at his tear. When the men
return from the sour fields, they
bow, kiss his hands, whatever,
and are ritually tongue-tied. Children
romp in the mud, shy or cheering,
and grandmothers, between blessings,
nag daughters and granddaughters,
making sure everyone is being a good cow.

There's not much here besides culture
but his house is full of food
they bring. There's a fan,
a TV. He watches awhile,
then sleeps. A woman
descends mysterious steps.
She's nude, strong-limbed, intelligent, full
of intent. The one time something
remotely similar happened
to him, he fled crazed.
But sleep gives him control.
He thinks, She's temptation, the void, a demon,
and I need only wake.
Or, A goddess come to reward me!
Or (unlikely) he thinks, She's real
and has nothing to do with me.

Costa Concordia

The ship, yellow, blue,
transparent and white,
like a toy; the divers
purposeful, pointless
in green haze; the aria
of the Guardia Costale:
Get back on the ship, Schettino!
Why aren't you on your ship?; even
cell-phone shots of pale,
packed faces
above orange life-vests, seeming
to listen for a scream,
and clips of screams in darkness ...
sublimely the future enters.
For a moment, through the Captain's
evasive gaze, an image,
almost redemptive,
of hulks rusting everywhere
in deserts.

Figure with Doll

The lines of sight, from door to chair
and from window and wall (walls can see,
if they look) to chair
are empty now, and safe;
though a fortress, some sort
of instant other wall,
would be more so, invisibility
more so, perhaps nothingness,
which must be another place.
The chair makes noise if one exists too much.
The window would see in if it were clean.
Silence decays. Only
one surface here has color
and lightness and absorbs; asks
fingers to heal and create,
and comfort it for being if not for living.

White House Talks
-July, 2011

The most rational man in the room
never sighs or rolls his eyes
or interrupts. He projects ideas.
He projects the idea
that folks have the right to
their ideas, and since all folks are
folks, all ideas, if sincere,
are ideas. Some folks, at most,
should remember concern
for others; he projects this idea.
But the other men in the room,
though they believe, of course, in folks, believe more
in freedom. Folks are folks
if they're free, and they want ever more
of it; march for it
on their hot lawns under signs that read
We love our chains. They themselves
(the other men in the room)
have never felt closer
to it; and so they interrupt,
roll their eyes, walk out. If money
were more overtly present in the room,
it would speak of the coolness
in the mountains, of children's and grandchildren's
weddings, of the need for calm and trust;
the whole tone would be different,
but they would know what it meant. Instead it
(money) crusts the window
like extra humidity. The rational man,
looking out at it, feels confident
it will back him rather than these yahoos,
and almost sighs, a courtesan among whores.

Stinkbugs

They can fly, but prefer not to.
The noise they make when flying is neither
the rebel yell of mosquitos nor the football cheer
of flies, but one of complaint.
They emerge from things.
Sit on walls, screens, plates, and ceilings like mini-black holes.
Their brains are small.
The smell they emit, when alarmed or crushed dead, is inorganic.
They wait to be crushed.
If you lift one, carefully, or several, in a paper towel
and drop them in a toilet, they clamber
gradually from under the paper towel
and swim. They don't drown fast.
Have no orifices.
Which is why insecticides won't work.
And nothing here
eats them. They will win by sheer numbers.

A far less pleasant fruit of global warming
and globalization than the blue-
streaked lizards everywhere now.
Who are decently afraid, and flee, and are therefore elegant.
Whom it is bearable to imagine breeding
or eating. They're assimilable.

"Even That Which He Hath"

A man with few friends and no way
to make more renounced,
one by one, those he had.
He told them, in accents
of psychological acumen,
what had always been wrong
with them, for him.
He spoke in that singsong
which knows it's intolerable and imitates patience.
They stared, too incensed
to want the last word,
and left. For the space of a block, a minute,
they might have been recalled;
then disappeared, as friends do,
without trace. But the issue
is why he did it. It's how one recaptures
youth, by its stupid gestures;
or summons and finally
disproves final rescue;
or lives the last chapters
of forgotten novels. As for where it occurred:
where else but those places
whose tables are never entirely clean,
whose food repeats on one, whose music
fulfills the reigning purpose of music,
to numb the staff and hurry the eaters.

Cure

When they awake, three days after
the procedure, they promptly sit upright,
to show themselves our equals, or in fear.
And unless the family that cut them off
when violence, theft, and filth grew too intense
survives and is there, it's us they see and talk to
first. However disoriented, they seldom
look for their carts or bags or squares of cardboard,
at most for trinkets that were always with them;
and are plainly glad of louse-free hair, white sheets
and teeth. Some ask if they're in heaven.
We run our tests: eye-hand, simple performance.
Some find it hard at first to concentrate
on voices undisturbed by other voices.
Then they worry where they'll have to go and what
to do, and some, what town or year it is;
then, invariably, they cry. But only one
in my experience said, "It came on early
with me. I never had a ... center,"
and stared at us with his new sharpness.
"We've given you," I told him honestly,
"something generic, liberal and benign;
you won't hurt anybody and can learn."
The patient, after a long pause, said, "OK."

Lady Snake from Shaky Lake

A new thing has entered
the canyon, so arid and far
from malls and developments that its
creatures had thought they were safe
from all but each other, and bland occasional
looks from the two-lane road.
But plants and animals have gods
too, as self-delighted,
self-willed and unaccountable
as those of men and stones. Not quite real,
she nonetheless shivers
the peeling red madrone,
violet wishbone bush and blue
lupins. A wave in the floor
of the canyon, she wears a flowery veiled
hat with a plume that would tickle her chin
if she had one, and screams
that the berries she smells would go right to her hips
if she had some, and smiles
at her prey as if letting them in
on a joke. She's immense. The males
who gather from mudholes are, in their low way,
besotted with her: she's
exotic! From elsewhere! But whether
their type boasts hemipenes or quadripenes,
she sends them squirming off
with funny, cutting words; sex,
unlike food, is for her immaterial.
Then she curves to the crest of the hill
among the bowing grasses, brandishes
herself like a spear, and addresses
the lives below, which, from
the somber beetles to the manic mice,
stop to worship and fear. She describes
an ocean, the lands bordering it,
the rock below those lands
shifting uncomfortably. And a great Sound
beneath the grasp of the keenest ear,
ringing from end to end
of the world until it's echoed here!

Here, she repeats, with that
joy assuming mutuality
with which an artist or a god exults.
As if they should feel proud
that the floor of their home will shear
and fire and water come. Yet all
remain respectful, though they wonder why
unaccustomed consciousness
had been evoked to end like this,
and the thing happens. Distant towers fall.

Hasty Orison

These faces of the slain –
first thousand in Afghanistan –
on TV with solemn music
(not pop for once) and taking up
four pages of the *Post* –
What can you do,

what's expected
apart from your own silence,
strange embarrassment,
and sense of multiple futilities?
Focus on one, then another,
with their statistics –

Sergeant, 40, Kansas,
Private, 19, Maine, a girl –
earnest or blandly smiling,
some apparently just in
from attending a game
with kids or parents,

keeping forever their own counsel,
Marine necks squeezed by dress blues.
But possibly you're being set up
to love them, as to hate
the ones who killed them, who wanted
only to herd goats, grow poppies,

beat women, screw boys, equate knowledge
with memorization, sustain vendettas,
and to be left alone?
Perhaps you think this, or that
de Maistre's apophthegm –
All did not die, but all were there to die –

doesn't play well in democracies.
Somebody set them up,
these photos. Like mugshots.
Or like an impossibly thorough,
centralized record
of the structurally unemployed. – Yes,

very like that.
They keep their own counsel. Some,
doubtless, were Oath Keepers,
reluctant to fight for a "Kenyan" commander-
in-chief. Some may have planned
to apply their explosives training

back home. But even they
are too polite to say so, now,
lined up for this group shot.
After which, R&R, from the rigors of
the uniform, tight or loose,
and war and being human.

Fable

In one of the late warm days
of empire, a girl gets off a bus.
She is concerned not only
with her patchwork luggage
and directions to carry it, but with not
submitting for a second to the pathos,
whoever may feel it, of a girl
alone, in a dress pre-worn and travel-worn.
Never asking for help
in her provincial accent, she makes her
way to her dorm. There, with only
a hint of ritual, she showers,
and unpacks in the better half
of the two-girl room. Then she locates
her faculty advisor, who is more
solicitous than she expected
or wants. And just before the banks
near campus close, she opens an account
with worn bills from a thick taped envelope.
By the time the other, younger
freshmen arrive and fill
the streets and campus with their noise,
she has found a job, making calls about loans,
and has bought a new pair of shoes.
When the first snow falls, she buys
a coat. By now she has noticed
library carrels abandoned
by upperclassmen on weekends, and studies there
all weekend. Her roommate finds her dull
but neat and unobtrusive;
and when the father appears,
the roommate says she doesn't know
where she hangs out. The father is drunk and smelly,
but leaves after extorting
several dollars "for the parking."
That summer the girl takes a room
off-campus, paid for in part
by her boss at the collection agency,
in part by a chinless married
clerk at the Student Aid Office.

She completes remedial
English and math, and in her sophomore year
declares her major, Bus. Ed.,
gets a job with hopes of promotion,
and dismisses one of her lovers.
Twice more the father visits. The first time
she manages to avoid him;
the second time he's on a sidewalk
in front of her, in winter. Demands
that she come home and help, asks how
she can completely abandon
the family, and hits her. By chance
a police car is passing.
He doesn't return. In later years,
in her luxury condo, she thinks
of him as if by appointment, rarely,
and with slightly less economy
of a dog and brother.

Gesture

Long after print, but not yet after words,
a survivor is led
to a podium. Mountains form
his backdrop, the usual
symbol of sublimity
now that the seas are slime, the prairies stone,
the universe too expensive.
He's cute: big-eyed, not too brown,
a post(er)-child. The reporters expect
the voice will be soft and high; the cameras eat
him up. The survivor
thanks the machines
that rescued him, and the people
who brought him to the beautiful mountains.
He tells how the sea,
which had already eaten
his country, broke
or went around the wall
raised against it. He describes
the latest fifty million
gently bobbing corpses
as if he knew them all. The reporters,
who scheduled only thanks
and some tears, start to edit. But the survivor
(his voice is high and soft and sad),
saying that neither
those deaths nor his presence here
were necessary, unbuttons
the shirt he has been kindly given.
Revealing not the explosive vest
of religion, but only himself,
which dissolves, becoming
wind and a virus.

Fauteuil

Old men, if they have any brains,
repress anger. For while
the anger of the young
serves life (at worst rearranging
its ugly features), that of the old
draws what energy it has
from death, and repays
with interest. Old women
regard old men's anger,
like their bellies and hair, as
abstractly forgivable.
(Their own is like housework,
a thing somewhat apart.)
Quiet old people lean
back in their armchairs,
doze perhaps, perhaps
consider how anger
is one letter away
from angel. A misprint
could slip towards that word.

Sigil

Few saw the painful scene,
but as staff led the perpetrator
away, the people in the restaurant
stared. They wanted to assure themselves
that their white ethnicity, round,
square, lumpy, borderline-brown,
or homogenized, was not his.
That their clothes
were not his, which were too rough,
too plaid, polyester, whatever
was wrong. Above all, that his eyes
and snarl could under no circumstances
be theirs, and that they were therefore safe
from evil or madness or
some worse, nameless thing.

His arms not actually held, he was
nonetheless being hustled, crowded
out. And as he yielded, under
patent though silent protest,
to this and began to walk,
he twirled a finger –
not at his temple, but over
his head, in a wide, articulated,
then narrowing spiral,
at the heavens beyond the tasteful lighting.

"Meeting a Madman at Night"

-Otto Dix, lithograph, 1916

Behind him the trench
is a path he made.
He looms between parapets,
despising, having completely forgotten
bullets. A severed tree
lies oddly, neatly;
a house writhes towards the moon
like, once,
its smoke. Things wait
to be reduced further,
are meanwhile lucent,
lucid. The night per se
is his bow-wake:
full dark on ribs beneath rag-flesh,
around the hash-mark smile, the cigarette eyes.
There is threat, certainly,
but not that he will speak.
At some distance, now, one can see
he is pleased and confident and will
survive. In a sense.

South Side

East of Midway, 55th
becomes two Garfield Boulevards,
a half-block park between.
In summer, at every intersection,
alone or in groups,
people sell bottled water.
They face the street, the burnt,
boarded and empty,
or barred and crowded apartments.
Wind from the cars lifts plastic bags
and paper from grass and sidewalks.
Kids shuffle towards basketball,
picnics, and dealers
in the park, are yelled back
by stick-limbed or very fat
grandmas in lawn-chairs
in the shade of trees, beside coolers.
The cars seldom stop,
whether all their windows
are down or up. Yet at the corner
of Normal, Ada, Throop, Racine,
Union, LaSalle, an arm waves
a bottle, a sweat-ringed mouth
calls. So that it seems
one person, and as if
repetition attempted
to say *I'm fulfilling a role,*
am needed, have purpose. No sale.

Suits

Their circumstances and chronology
gone, suits migrate
in memory, become composite
or imagined, but never leave.
Item: a pinhead, looking thus
because his head is shaved, muscles vast
under the suit; he's smart enough
to do what he's paid for and loves: to replace
expression with menace
and aim it at you. A noble-haired, regretful
professional, face sagging
lower onto the suit with every
penalty he issues: *this hurts me more*
than it does you (perhaps, but he loves pain).
And one who regrets
only what time of his
you waste, and with barely a glance
decides the remainder of
your time; his suit
is sharp. There are others, staring, compiling
reports; some, comparatively harmless, red-faced
and shouting, some no doubt resembling
you. It's fanciful
to think the lapel-pins
you notice towards the end, at
a distance, are more than mere
flags, that they are in fact
the secret symbol of man, the man you weren't.

Petting Zoo

You can't hold adult
koalas. "They're brutal,
awake," grinned the keeper.
"Scream and bite,
get tossed off branches.
Doesn't quite fit the image?"
Instead a baby,
clutching a mama-sized
doll. Eyes tightly,
bulgingly closed, as if learning.

Then, in a wide dusty
pebbly region, a wallaby
lying on its side. Something
of a cat's turn of the head,
a cat's look, but with
an athlete's, not an aesthete's boredom.

The wombats, bowlegged
behind a widely-woven fence,
looked rudimentary.
Lego in furs. I liked them.
One chewed,
heavily, my thumb, wondering
if I was a mushroom.

They all felt like Velcro.

Troll

For once, let us libtards
("liberal retards") not
speculate whether
the world around him
is a basement, a crazed abusee
bustling their kids off
to church, his mother, or
fellow despairing salesmen
at some forsaken dealership. When
he opens his computer
and clicks on an enemy
site, he's no longer
whatever stereotype we,
however justly, imagine. He's
a knight, defending
what everyone knows
against our science. First on the scene
beneath the articles, he chips away
at our lies. For every ten
scandals we mention, he can name one
of ours. For every hundred
fatcats. His passion
rises until he can type
the precious word "stupid"
about us. And while
he works, for love, for nothing, he's
the Creator of Wealth,
the superior man, wealth
itself. The moral arc
of the universe is short and bends towards him.

Clinic at Night

Laptops are closed or home.
On older monitors, screen-savers
mutate from multicolored box to sphere
to spiky ball, trampolining
the borders of their world.
Red LEDs, and the numbers
of the security pad, glow comfortably.
Clean paths have been traced in the clean carpet;
the desks are places one would like to be.
Where files are material, where they contain,
say, pictures too heavily crayoned,
they have been locked away. The pictures
in the waiting-room, above the toys
and big and little chairs, sleep
as well as only smiling
stick-people can, the box-house, the archetype.

Doors have been left half-open
for the same reason pictures
are tilted, in homes, by maids. The windows
and one-way mirrors shine
in meager light. Only the doll's-house
in one of the offices seems
disorderly, behind its missing wall:
figures lying or standing where they shouldn't,
small furnishings strewn or broken.
Does no one neaten the dolls?

Odor

Like a garden gnome, but indoors, and
without the usual cute belligerence
or faint allusion
to gargoyles. Twisted,
gray, stuck off against
a wall; some sort of statement

amidst what is all otherwise
charming. Or at least comfortable
to a casual eye, livable
despite austerity –
lines of sight converging
tactfully on a crucifix,

a narrow bed, some shelves
of sacred texts in learned
deshabille. (Why should austerity
be prickly?) And flowers, flowers –
almost overwhelming
each surface, and the sill

of an open window: pollen-
coated from within
and without, a sweet breeze lifting
the thin lace and bringing,
forever from the playground
outside, the voices of boys.

View of the Water

Beyond the retaining wall,
the sea is unusually clear:
outlines of buildings, stubs of docks,
the unrecoverable streets
all visible from here,
colloidal bubbles rising here and there.
It looks like the clients
have decided to take three apartments
on the fiftieth floor, remove walls. The agent
stands with them on a balcony.
The air is fresh, the mood
relaxed in the way that comes
when drawbacks and their costs have been agreed
and postures put aside,
and parties are briefly one
in their reluctance to proceed
with the day. The agent sinks
into his native observant heaviness.
He could have asked for more.
They aren't suffering.
The wife seems marginally
more alert. Both are on something,
and in that fancy sungear
can hardly be told apart.
Not merely rich but connected, they travel,
know other cities. He wonders whether
they see him as part of local color
and how they'd react to what he lives in.
The husband checks the time in his brain.
The realtor straightens, looks down
at puddles beneath
the wall and scuttling
people the size of rats the size of men.

Figure

Though historical references may seem
superfluous here, it was a time
before the working class was eased
from the illusory middle class and both dissolved.
Color televisions played
behind the heavy oak apartment doors,
and one could also hear
between parental bellows the increasingly
distinct and lucrative music
of the young. The stairwell
was still occasionally cleaned, new cabbage
and burnt casserole smells
layered upon those lingering from the war.
And the man climbing climbed
slowly, already old-in-waiting, with
his own unexceptional tang
of cigars, a smile for hurtling,
noisy, still potentially literate
children, and eyes avoiding those
of adults whom he might or might not meet.
Perhaps he was a "premature anti-fascist,"
never now to be rehired
at the level of his training, pride, or,
God knows, ideals. Or a former SS-man,
with a fanciful and touching
new past, as safe as he could hope.
Or merely someone lonely.

Without

How often I've wanted to write something
without symbols and with only the flimsiest
metaphors. Then buses, pills, dogs and leaking
pipelines would at last be themselves,
without aura, seen as fleas, spreadsheets, and they
themselves see. Viewed without finicky,
ever-doubtful ever–improvised detachment,
but from the same sort of head, stuffed
with the same sort of mucus as anyone's.

A shrink – he was a Jungian and had
his reasons – said when I was thirty
that such an art, like a ripped balloon,
wouldn't get off the ground. Whether we view
time as a metaphor, or timeless moments, timeless
truths (like what he said), what he said
was true. We may regard, therefore,
this poem, like any poem about poetry
or the poet's hesitations, as dead for eternity.

As such it sails, like a ghost galleon
or Marie Celeste, past my friend Mike
in Berkeley, heroic aging activist
who, unprovoked on a recent visit, said
"In however small a way one can always act"
(or "must," whatever). I mentioned neither
inertia, illness, fear, nor impacted
self-flattering despair but nodded,
partly in pious agreement, partly with tact.

It also, or the prosaic and sullen
theme it bears, sails, or let's say crawls
past Mike's constituents, housed in the faith
and packing cases of the upper class,
endlessly stringing Styrofoam beads. Oh
there is ecstasy (say better clarity or sleep)
in knowing that you cannot help or punish
anyone; the knowledge is like wind
in a poem's sails or up its ass.

It's autumn, after protracted summer.
Brown facts fall on brown lawns.
I have an image of a kind of palace
with many balconies, in a landscape farmed
by robots. I haven't filled it
with anyone yet. What matters
is the breeze, which would have to remain
sweet. It's a compensatory fantasy
and nobody's business. Like a business.

North Tampa

Mud daubers base their nest
in the darkness under the eaves
on a paralyzed spider the young eat.
They work in mud, paper wasps in something
like paper. Palmetto bugs,
seeking the sweetness of fruit and hair
and their own or related dead,
enter. There is no outside, no
inside unless defined
by the vulnerable coolness
of rooms, steady innocence
of television, the music
thrashing somewhere the pool of the street.

Who would not seek, then, a right
turn out of jungle onto
the boulevards that are themselves
the highest species? Breeding, extending
space against termite time?
Breeding and feeding themselves
on chains that offer grits, wings,
sports, the sweetest beer,
or things of an assumed
higher class; and clinics, and billboards
endorsing clinics, where
presumably pedestrians are.
The swelling boarded windows themselves

are offspring, a brand. All names are brands.
At night there are only names,
glowing like algae, and crosses.
Directions among the hundreds
of boulevards seem nominal
despite numbers. One
would have to know them, like
the police cars that pause
at eddies in the shallows
to graze; or, in the greenish searing
dawn, the old man
in wool with a sign
protesting the murder of the unborn.

Summer

The unthrill of a summer room
with, for some reason (poverty,
economizing, perverse taste), no a/c,
the pointillist desperation
of birds, the war of all
against nature interpreted
(with long breaks) by leafblowers, and
a truck (that being of distances!)
alone audible, leaving
room for the subdued unsubtle
counsels of close heat: that
effort was never commensurate
to challenge, that self flakes
like skin and has been doing so
a long time, that language cannot
justify anything and the "still small voice"
is inane.

Ice

If you stand long enough
by the ice in the crosswalk,
seeking without success
a way round,
shadows will come. They will take you by the arms
and guide your tremulous feet
to safe places. Then, facing
the hard, jagged snow
between you and home, they'll say, *This can't*
be allowed. And more shadows
will emerge from houses
you never quite noticed
along the way, to clear it.
You'll want to thank them; and, peering
directly at them, see
not shadows but thick
stalwart men, strong willowy wives, a motif
of plaid wool. (Though should
you look away they'd be shadows again,
so you don't.) It's far
to your house, even on new-swept
sidewalk, and lonely;
when it comes, you've no reason
to refuse their invitation.
An impromptu party fills
a living-room, with a fire
against the dark noon.
There are paintings of ships under sail,
red textured wallpaper, cats,
demure but interested children,
antique tools and an air of tools
that work. So many cars,
you're told, have landed in snowdrifts
they have banished cars from the street,
and are leaving theirs to dissolve into ore.
While winter lasts, they walk en masse
to the supermarket; but
come spring there will be cows and vegetables
in the joined, fenceless yards. And if spring
is late, they will send expeditions

to settlements across
the half-admitted, half-forgotten
city. Someone plays guitar.
Here and there in the house
are traces of flute. You sip
homemade cordial, quite good, and say
how happy you are
they found you, how much you intend
to do your thoughtful, small, debilitated
bit. But now a young man,
increasingly edgy and visible
among them, attacks. Is this
what you dream of, afraid and old
before a patch of ice? This
reactionary niceness? And what is
the theme? The dregs of utopian longing,
or death? Have the two become one,
does it come to that?
He *will* not accept it! You turn
your rheum-closed eyes
away, as if needlessly apologizing
for him to the shades, or as if ashamed.

Spring's Awakening

In the '70s, New Yorkers rode
the subway surrounded and
depressed by downscale art.
Cars looked like intestines. Transit officials
loved the ensuing war
for civilization, cleanliness,
property. They loved its futility,
its *Götterdämmerung* spirit, and hated their
foe with an intensity
later reserved for Moslems. They scoured
and hosed metal panels, installed
new metal panels, which
attained from any angle
and in every light the look
of an incised vortex. (All matter
will end in a vortex. There are cancers that,
while killing the host, infect themselves.
Some tapeworms lay their eggs in their own bodies.)
Taggers meanwhile

evaded the barbed wire
around yards, the cops, the third rail.
Were crushed sometimes. Clung,
if need be, to the sides of moving trains.
Which they filled inside and out
with their art: the stoned colors and
phat 3-D zigzags
of streets and names. Proclaiming,
said curators later,
authentic underclass rebellion. Till

three unembellished black
letters, a name,
began to be sprayed
over theirs: **CAP**. It appeared all
over town. Not large, but annihilating.
CAP put a cap
on beauty. He just a fool, he got no right,
said the artists, almost crying.
But wasn't he courageous also,

daring the same tunnels? And doesn't
envy or self-hatred have
a right to self-expression?

Waiting Room of a Therapist

It's underground, a "Lower Level."
Four white doors, a coffee table
with old New Yorkers, and a box
of Kleenex, as if people
started crying here.
The schedules change, are not in sync.
A former football player
in his expensive suit
hurries out at noon
perhaps to his psychiatrist
(which now means pill-dispenser).
The next month he's absent,
and the most ancient shrink
mumbles in at 12:10
a cadaverous hair-twister.
Only the old lady
with her fussiness or dignity
is regular; the office
she enters seems intensely underlit.
We have no solidarity.
Even chemo might allow
more humor, more eye-contact.
Somebody might wish
to comment, at least
on the weather topside,
but the desire breaks
against the white-noise generator.

Ashbery

This wallpaper and I are fighting a duel to the death.
Either it goes or I do. – Oscar Wilde, *last words*

Towards the end of the Mallarméan Project,
at the dawn of postliteracy and the Modular Icon,
as Fordist gave way to speculative
then oligarchic capital,
at the corner of Fifth and 47th just
above the future shoreline, on
a beautiful spring morning Ashbery walked.
Sincere amateur of Eighties Figuratism,
gracious exponent of Wheelwright, David Schubert
and other outriders, central poet
and all-around nice guy,
he observed fellow stakeholders,
pullulating on that corner,
with a distanced benevolence. As if,
in another world, anything would be possible –
even the Habermasian
"Ideal Speech Situation"!
Little did they realize
that within him pronouns
promiscuously merged,
that the odalisques of high and the lowest art
shlupped each other, past present future
kowtowed to the anomic drooling
conditional, that the very air they breathed
was up in the air! But the Lacanian Real,
beyond the border of the myths and puns
we call real, owns police –
a SWAT team. Like force,
they plunged from their black sudden vehicle,
like things they stood in their stunning armor
around him. And as they disappeared
Ashbery, he was heard to cry,
"I only wanted to make peace with the wallpaper."

83

Dream of Fair Women

A space of vaults and curves, diffuse
forgiving light, and flowers.
With nothing at all
of a Lautrec brothel
breakfast or Ingres harem.
History is the history
of fashion, progress is comfort,
and the women
have settled on the styles of 1920:
Fortuny, Lanvin. A demure
androgynous android serves coffee.

One might think their leader,
queen or facilitator,
would be someone like the wife
Faludy lost to cancer
between the Hungarian labor camp
and poverty in America:
I hold a tattered rope, pathetic arm.
It slides from my hand ...
But no. Like other distant stars,
kissed in notebooks
buried in death-march mud or prison lime,

she's content to enjoy
the rivalry among
the Romans – Lesbia, Cynthia, Delia –
out of control for millennia,
a circus. Even the proud
abstracted loves of later Europe,
with names like alchemical spells, yield
to *them*. How much more
reserved, then, the "she"s
and "you"s who structure poems
for modern bourgeoisies:

nameless, told at length
what they once did and said,
how they slept, moaned, turned away
and what it meant,
by him who wrote. The ladies seldom recall

the words that got them
into this club. Rather walk in the garden, garden,
play cards, *read* cards – the dark
mysterious stranger,
the one who will come, remains
a source of interest and hilarity.

Then to herald each lavish
supper and sunset,
a voice from a charming
sort of minaret
in the distance calls itself to prayer:
"*Your breasts defined all softness,*
your scent all nature,
your lips all kindness, your kindness
the purpose of my strength, the goal of time."
But the silence
that follows mostly seems to defer response.

At night they write back.

The Castle

Someone, impossibly,
on the far hills who gazed
at this House and its surroundings,
would find them uninviting;
what matters is they're mine.
He wouldn't see that. Nor, except
for a few wind-taxed trees,
the life of this place, which lurks
in burrows or above them;
spreads, luxuriantly poisonous,
in pools; coats and absorbs stone.
Flees or pursues,
that flicker replacing
shadow in the sunless days. No one who,
impossibly, lived
thoughtfully here could fail to discern
evolution, or that what it
perfects remains prey.

That unlikely observer might offer
cigars, binoculars, but nothing
coherent, a way of life,
and so does not attract.
And if I crossed the waste, I might
confront, in a manner of speaking,
people: troglodytes, outlaws.
They would be deferential, faceless;
would tug their locks and their hair would fall out,
their flesh fall off and resolve into mud,
which would grow knives to stab me as I passed,
which is the other face of deference.
And if I reached that hill, I'd have to
show pride, impassiveness, interest, hauteur,
civility, in a manner of speaking.

So I'm better at home, avoiding views.
Though the wind at once
besieges and breaks through
walls, the sullen food
resists digestion, spidered chandeliers

swing from vaults
like censers at the obsequies of light.
Of the stained glass nothing remains
but a gesture, part of a shield,
clotted heraldry;
the allegory floats free
of meaning but won't stoop to metaphor.
It rewards thought, the way
long expeditions through these halls
contain others. Empty complete suits
of armor, my companions,
may be no match for modern weapons,
but the sword retains its virtue. Its edge.

In the Hallway

A girl pressing her cheek against a door,
doorjamb, or wall beside a door.
Crying probably, possibly
mumbling. That's it.
Her face is turned away,
you can't see if she's pretty.
Which would make a difference
in your quotient of empathy
divided by reluctance
to get involved plus eventual impatience.
And if and how quickly
you escaped the sense
of not being a plausible
savior (someone she'd find
attractive when this is over), or –
long-cherished, firmly-held –
of helplessness. A novelist
cases the hallway, the smells and light,
social class as revealed
by her dress. Or should.
For my part, I (not making this
about me) check
the decaying file, the yellowed partial volume
of memory. Not finding her.
But she exists now, therefore always did
and will, and is both punishment and forgiveness.

In Van Nuys

A quadriplegic since childhood,
he imagined and someone placed
a stalk on his helmet,
to which chalk
of various lengths and colors
could be more or less easily
attached. He had the
knack of moving his head
deliberately and little, although
drool fell continually. When
he completed not merely
two or three
lines to his satisfaction but a
passage, he made the *delighted* sound –
howw-HAAA-ow –
and changed chalks
with absolute attention, ignoring meals.

On cardboard, six by five: animals
predating the division
between dog and cat,
in forests, yellow-eyed.
Sometimes a woman, one curve
of hair and back, immense, smiling,
the breasts a single breast,
the creative arm hinted.
Gold skin and black brow,
the creatures reflecting.
No other world during the work-time,
a month each. At least, his
attendant said he said "No other world."
I think the one I bought
is beautiful, but there's always
a problem in justifying that.
In translating.

Better

Massively he leans over her.
Her eyes are sunken but her gaze is love.
Her hand on his has no more force
than the breath that whispers "no";
she means it, but can't avert the kiss.

Immediately her breathing eases,
color returns; she begins to sit up,
but must expend that strength on tears.
Pale and small, he can no longer
hear her. Or express his joy.

Landscape near an Idea

Moss of a darker green
than all the surrounding
meadow or the forest beyond that
fills the inscriptions – regular, severe,
in no decipherable language –
on widely scattered stones. It seems
to be reading, trying to emphasize,
but only erases them.
Perhaps an expert touch
can make those letters come
from the future, not the past,
and thus suggest more pathos, bear
more truth to some.

The weather is warm or cool,
nothing intrusive. A city
beyond the hills may be required,
or the absorption of all cities
by their own cruelty, time, or
other abstraction.
The nearest slope resembles a woman's
hip. She's comfortable there,
a languid giant out of Baudelaire,
yet might be happier
human-sized, running nude
through scrub. It's entirely
at the viewer's discretion.

Because there is no privacy.
To think is to be perceived.
Above the grass, insects rise
and descend, in place, in the air.
They are, that is they become
viewers, their focus
inevitably obscured
by a mist. As they push towards it,
they see a tacky reproduction
of the thinker. That can't be right,
some realize, their clamor
filling the silence, their movement
creating fences in that openness.

Charisma

As he spoke, the IQ
of his class diminished.
When he reached the tenth minute
they had forgotten five.
As he finished that sentence
they lost its beginning.
When he started the next,
they would have been texting
if he had not forbidden
"gadgets." And as
his periods became
more classical ("convoluted,"
they would have said
if they could still speak), more
subtle, judicious
and synergetic, they could
think only of bodies,
sun and beaches,
beer, their debts,
neurotic obsessions,
and of that grail of students,
sleep. And as the kindly,
insightful voice droned on,
they saw a bridge
to the end of their lives,
all monies earned and spent, the final
wheelchairs, talk-shows, rage.
He was pleased, justifiably,
with the lecture, although
he knew he had lost them;
which matters, finally,
less than lucidity.

Observation

Bores of the nice, i.e.,
non-ideological type
are *empiricists*. The material
that went into the rug
had enough left over
to cover chairs in the basement.
A place in one mall,
though owned by a relative, had
nothing; likewise the second,
renowned, in another mall;
but the third offered a sofa
of the proper magnitude, whiteness,
and resistance to stains.
Things can be found on consignment
and friends escort one to them. Or to
games. Friends are professionals,
have houses and problems
that require other professionals.
The place of value in a world of fact
is contingent, auxiliary. Meanwhile,
whereof one cannot speak one must be silent.

The Element of Surprise

At room temperature
it is a fine yellow powder
like sulfur, without the smell.
Like one of the less effective
pet-safe insecticides,
fairy dust, pollen from
the *Urpflanz*, anthrax spread
in corners by the subtlest terrorist.
Breathe deep, go outside,
and flowers will seem spectacularly
flowers, superpredators children,
life a miracle and capitalism life
enough to base a mainstream poem
or religious bestseller on.
You might even see a stranger
across a crowded room.

Patton believed in tactical,
not geostrategic surprise.
He wanted to push the Third Army
straight across France to Berlin. Ike,
however, worrying about supplies,
refused. Later, at Ohrdruf,
Ike snapped at Patton
because, among piles of Jews,
he kept making wisecracks. Well, he was nervous.
These things happen.
The point was to keep one's eye
steadily on the inevitable
war with communism, arm in arm
with a somewhat reformed Wehrmacht.
Nothing surprises the wise.

You go out. Yellow drifts
rise in the wind and reclump.
Death will arrive in stages,
which, after a certain point,
you grasp. Your fellow passersby
are sorry you feel that way.
Their indifference, that of things at large, and

order in a little park
between buildings may afford
epiphanies but no surprise.
Buses pass with ads
for you; it is your music everywhere,
your face or something like it on the billboards.

House of the Bogeyman

1

The *Old Musician*
of Manet, fresh from its niche
at the National Gallery, is carried
professionally, silently,
through the arch of my Great Room
by the team that heisted it –
still, always, in black ski-masks and their black,
light-bending, antigravitic tights.
Ever-silent, they hang it,
obeying my hissed commands
and laser pointer, in the right relation
to the Kiefer and Frankenthaler,
the Corot and the middle-period de Kooning
(you can see it, can't you? See the colors, the rightness?).
But this happens
as always, necessarily, in darkness,
as well as, as I've intimated, silence.
Only moonlight daubs
gold frames, pearled monstrances, stained glass.
My eyes long since adjusted; I perceive
echoes of shapes, a downward transposition
of tones. Still, it seems limiting ...
One day I'll have to multiply the moon.

2

To me the night is merely where I walk,
seeing by sonar
hallways that narrow, widen, turn
cunningly to create
repeated impressions of a goal.
Sconces, mica and marble,
loom for appearance's sake;
if lit, they would defeat
the purpose. It took considerable empathy
to understand fear
of the dark. Which for me is ... frictionless:
each shadowed sofa

and spidered stairwell only reassures.
Sometimes I pause
beside doors. From within come sighs, cries,
shrieks, moans of all sorts –
all signifying, I gather, troubled sleep.

3

Light, forty watts, is reserved for serious things
in my inaccessible study,
whose disorder alarms even me.
Though I choose not to think
that in themselves these ceiling-storming piles
make me a "hoarder"; only,
the window seems unreasonably remote.
Here I keep up with cosmology.
Current theory is that the Big Bang
was no big deal because the sum
of negative energies cancels out
the others … Something
is basically nothing, in other words.
There's a corollary
that cheers me: that the final cold and dark
will be suitable for development,
like a city of vacant lots. Like Detroit,
which remains a "city" though it dissipates.
Something will use the space where space was; something,
if only poison oak, will use Detroit.

4

My dreams (or nightmares, though I doubt the distinction)
occur by contrast in sunlight.
One part of me's a Captain, another a Sergeant,
and we're on an old stomping-ground;
but since time turns and turns again
in sleep, we're under a new flag.
At our feet is a local
who threw acid in the faces
of girls who had formed a school. We're here to punish him.
"Gender equality
threatens most viscerally
the regressive/patriarchal genome," says the captain.

"The desert is poisoned, as well as 50° C,"
says the sergeant. "I'm barely functional."
"Effective, unified, progressive action
was prevented by the fact
that our positions were *rational*, not, like those
of our enemies, psychotic. One becomes ill to win."
"Freedom is almost visible when the dust
is settled by scarce oil or scarcer water."
Thus Sarge. "I miss my partner," sighs Cap.
"We live with punctilio, a *meum et tuum*
as strained as that of fundamentalists,
but fun." The prisoner emits medieval
curses. We gag and beat him. "The limits of tolerance
are crossed when the tolerated
inflicts *for whatever reason* pain on the helpless
or deprives her of access to full culture."
One of us says that. "When we're done here,
will we finish the job at home, or what's left of it?"
"There are so many lampposts in the world
and all so lonely." "Rrg rrg rg rrrg rrg rrrrg
rrg rrg rrr!" says the captive,
or words to that effect. "Sometimes when I gaze
at the waste, I have a vision of a forest
built by our love, and a gray sky." –
I envy creatures who dream narrative.
I weary of my fragments, and awake.
Leave them contemplating acid.

5

If drugs, an under-the-blanket
Xbox, or the lack
of an actual bedtime don't help (or, in your case,
apply), and you stare
at the door of a closet, a weird cupboard,
or mentally under the bed,
and scream for one or, less likely, both
your parents to come back because
I'm there and may at any point emerge –
know this. In whatever closet, cave,
or singularity you fear, there isn't
one presence but two. If you want
you can call them the Good and the Bad Guy, although

that complicates matters. And however
grotesque you imagine one of them
(say me) to be, the other
is equally, though piquantly, contrastingly
gross. And they are at each other's throat,
groin, eyes, forever, the noise
of struggle absorbed by struggle. And therefore I
will never come for you, fangs dripping, or even
weeping. And you may safely enter
sleep, which is (though it would take some time
to explain this) an enormous current
opposite time, and rest assured
your mommy and daddy love you very much.

6

There is, in the territory
I've marked, a ruin; and when
lightning like the bloodshot veins
and thunder like the tummy-rumbles
of a god fill the murk, I like
to ooze out there. In former times,
the fat and smudgy fonts
of rugged individuals, purveyors
of tight shoes and snake-oil, faced
the solid stones of shops.
These fell to rubble, were
absorbed by cities, which are also markets,
and which eventually missed and
rebuilt them; but this time
in Styrofoam and laminate,
with speedy corporate typefaces.
Which made in turn the ruin I enjoy:
a field of papier-mâché
and running ink, with occasional twisted
vertebrae of rebar under the rain.
You'd think that, blatant Romantic that I am,
I'd long for arches, obelisks, stone, stone,
but I prefer this.

Via Negativa

1

As they entered, they found that saints,
candles, virgins, gold
altar cloth, flowers, the cross and the figure
on it were gone, the never-comfortable
chairs folded in shadow. The pulpit
would no more frame a priest who might
have been a pederast and fascist
or, who knows, a liberal, full of doubt and thought;
hopefully now exercising
his virtues elsewhere, having lost his office.
They stood examining the effect
of unstained light on stone, of air
laden only with time, and how
the least sound echoed oddly in that room.

All were distressed; some stood in groups to pool
ignorance, some groundlessly
accused others. But the silence was too vast
and unfamiliar to them: that of a void
which concentrates the larger void.
It wore them down, though an old woman cried
at length, and only because crying
was familiar. Finally they could hear
their inner promptings from a distance
wide enough for names: greed, willful
stupidity, inadequacy ... Staring
across that gap at mirror-bright selves,
they hoped those noises too would end
and they be worthy of the greater silence.

2

Here and there, aging people
cherish untimely
ideals. They believe in

but seldom proclaim
the mild, benign State.
For the tired say

as little about the truth
as about the fun
they had in youth.

So they live. While those
who maintain forever
traditional hate

for one group or another
often live likewise; they
cheer but avoid

violence. At times
it occurs to the former
that they would give up

hope, if the others
relinquished desire
for cruelty. Then all

could be grains of sand
beneath a pale sky
on a calm land.

Portal

Those armed and glaring forms,
seeming guardians
that deputize for mountains
on either side of the gorge,
reveal no origin, yet one may sense
their why and whence. They were evil
forbidden to act
by some enormous spell,
which made no other mark,
displays no energy,
but leaves it to its object
to petrify and swell.

What Else Is New?

The suffering of others is a cake
that I will have to eat, though my teeth are a mess
and its lower layers are compressed
to stone by those above,
which extend out of sight and are always,
of course, rising. It's walled with florettes
of sugar and has different flavors,
all equally cloying. So, an eternity
of puking, though I take my time;
and insulin shots, and every systemic
ill before I reach
the inedible icing I caused.

Notes for an Opera

In the last act, wife and husband,
dirt poor, act out
an old Jewish joke.
"Why should we scrape and scrimp all our lives?
Make blintzes tonight!" He speaks this;
but from her "So, we can afford butter now?"
on, the orchestra bombards them
with minimalist arpeggios.
D for his "You'll make them *without* butter!"
F# for her "There's a bag of sugar
in the barn, suddenly?"
and so on through the cooking.
All major-key, *fortissimo*;
sax and electronics
like a disco ball (the lights likewise
around the hovel). Their phrases over and over;
exaggerated delivery;
the music jiggles the marionettes.
Short tuba-blast and rimshot at the punchline.

No, no. Low strings and oboe.
Clarinet, but not a hint
of klezmer! Neither anachronism
nor time. A "developing variation";
dissonant, wife's and husband's
repartee constrained, but the winds reaching
always for resolution.
"We'll make them without sugar."
"Without jam." "With one egg."
Tenderness, and exhaustion
throughout her stirring and baking;
that tiny flame reflected on the wall
sinks. It must smile, but not he –
he looks merely bemused
as he sings, "For the life of me, Chava,
what do people see in blintzes?"

Fourth Wall

A gentle species succeeds ours
at the top of a much-depleted nature.
They're satisfied to rid
their windowless cubes
of the enormous, cunning bugs;
to repel crow attacks,
and giant snakes
(that rise from the Car Layer and would
inspire new religions if they could).
And cleanse with stubby claws
their angular lanes
of tumbleweed and lacy undegradables.
Hate grids and production;

hate much, the sky above all;
but introject bile
and chew it throughout long phlegmatic lives.
Their art is a few lines,
poetry private, they're not hinged
for dance, and can't imagine theater:

to let someone decide
speech, and, worse, be entertained
by fate? Put one of them
onstage, it would hobble off,
enraged. As we should have.

View of the Lot

The broad, bare, glossy, neoclassical
desk invites creation,
even from one who lacks
a laptop, or one of the elfin,
excited gadgets that succeed them,
or skill at profiting
through those machines
from numbers that flicker invisibly, everywhere
around us. What else, however
(one who possessed
that skill might ask), could one "create" here?
The clawfoot armchair, green like the carpet,
suggests a break between bouts of trading.
But now the sun excessively warms
the chair's plush, one side
of the desk, and the floral spread
of the second bed. Below the window
an SUV leaves, another seeks
a slot nearer
the door. An old couple
approaches the decorative woods,
the level gravel path looping
a third of a mile; do they mean, arm in arm,
to walk? A car bleeps:
she settles him, straps him in, and drives away.
To crack the window the few permitted
inches would be to admit
uncanny heat, which has greyed
the trees and sears
JFK Boulevard, Nimitz Boulevard, the
developments and "campuses"
of this remote and abstract district.
The air-conditioning resumes as if
aggrieved. With the rubbery curtains
half-drawn, the room reduces
to a convex gleam
in the dark flat-screen. Such wealth
in there, of reasonably-priced
porn and bad movies, enough for weeks. Below, the mini-bar:
not all foods, admittedly, but something

like orange juice, a local wine,
and the peanut butter in crackers
connect with the vegetal world. A life
of sorts would be possible
briefly, enviably
cool. But now Housekeeping knocks
with a Spanish so polite as to sound panicked.
The used bed needs new sheets,
the other room many fresh towels
and soaps. In the lobby, the spoor
of kids and the waffle machine
has been replaced by Lysol and all-day coffee.
There is a basket of apples.
A woman hugs the computer.
The sun makes the sliding-glass door
of the entrance a wall. The concierge incuriously smiles.
She has seen, young as she is,
enough of life to know
it distributes people purposelessly, randomly.

Breath of Air

Someone was there in the night.
Gone now. So as not
to distract him, perhaps,
or tempt or shame him into relationship.
Am I ashamed? he wonders.
Is solitude still voluptuous?
He could make inquiries; roam
the corridors in search of her,
if that's the price ...
Has the time come for gentle melancholy?
Instead he showers. Breakfast
awaits when he emerges,
as always. In response
to subtle measurements of need
and mood, it consists
today of perfect eggs and sausages
beside the usual perfect bread.
He might like a newspaper –
there is probably news somewhere –
but finds, again, he's glad
to trace the variations of morning
from the river to the snow
on the peaks above it, glaciers and hawks
above those, the sea beyond and around
the mountains.
The window, as vast as the view, copies its curve,
and every day he reads the view like news.
Then he turns to the book, in thin leather,
that shares his table. Its characters suffer
as much as his imagination
permits, and will triumph, finally,
beyond his boldest hunch.
So he hopes. Each day he works,
and words arrange
themselves in stately print on the fine paper.
Though actually things haven't been going well,
even before the distraction of
last night. Blankness reclaims.
He needs some notes.
They're in his room back in town.

And a talisman, in a drawer of a dusty bureau.
So he dresses and leaves. The corridors
jog so as to avoid
oppressive endlessness. Are as inviting
as the suites, with nooks and landings looking
out on a variety of grandeurs.
Far ahead someone waves, disappears.
The writer wonders if politeness requires
he seek out his host. Of course not;
he can stay, leave and return
forever. The will of guests is absolute.
Beyond the majestic door,
the wind can't decide
between the early bite of spring and fall.
It is as pleasant as reviews
that say you have crystallized your times, or time.
He rests on a bench on a wooded ridge.
Before him the land slopes away.
Hills compensate for mountains; lakes,
receding to the horizon, for the sea
behind him. In however many days,
his ocher town,
static, sullen, cowed by space, escapable,
will rise on its dry plain.
But now the breeze changes, contains
a doubt. What if words
are really, loathsomely, equal,
fit to be thrown
by anyone, changed anyhow –
as if by a magician, barely attempting
to conceal the fraud – on some sort of screen?
What if there is no hierarchy, no patron?
Almost he doesn't dare to look back,
for fear he will have nowhere to return.
Almost the immensities he assumes
on every side collapse to leave
some filthy street ...
Then he shrugs and rises, swings his arms
as he descends into the day.
The moment becomes merely an experience.
For in that universe I, the host,
keep ambiguity and irony

in my vaults; what reaches for them,
and that from which it extends, are happiness.

Drink to That

Sunset; a bland, composite skyline
that empties onto prairie, veldt, and steppe.
Pedestrians, once turbulent and violent,
here fearful, hurrying home.
The mirror behind the bar reveals
a mouth pursed by the sharpest sweetness
or memory of pain.
You know this is the wrong eternity;
the knowledge guarantees you will remain.

Holland Island

-Chesapeake Bay

What's unclear from the story
is whether *he* took the photo
in which he says the child appears
by her grave, where she had told him
not to forget her, sinking with the others
into the silt. And what

his purchasing that house,
the last on the drowning island,
was meant to accomplish. But one
can grasp his thinking, here; in fact
it takes an effort not to.
All the rest was

predictable: split sandbags,
the bulldozer, plank breakwater,
and tons of wasted rock. It's unclear
what the wife felt, whether she's alive,
and how a former minister
might otherwise spend

his first fifteen years of retirement …
Finally, waves through the kitchen,
gulls on the collapsed roof,
chemotherapy on the mainland;
a monument to something unintended;
the graves just visible at low tide.

2012

Heat is the new cold. The creepers
investing every vertical
are frost; the ever-larger
lizards ranging ever farther
north, the reality
of trolls. The mutating insects
repeat the well-known phenomenon
of black specks on snow, which appear
with hypothermia, meteors,
and coal. As glaciers
recede, the bare rock
they leave has the authority
the glaciers once possessed.

Only for us is the difference
insuperable, woeful. We thought cold
would triumph and that one would have
a chance to fight. Giants,
the big wolf, the serpent
below and around things.
Die like a man, keep fires lit.
Instead, when the sun hits
the top of the pyramid, the carved
and painted kings
we thought we had escaped, with feather crowns,
and jade in their lips, and the scar
in their tongues, and blood-red arms
and that glare,
sufficiently heated, rouse themselves
and descend. To where we,
suddenly uniformly small and faceless,
have gathered, prostrate from heat,
which becomes prostration from submission.

The Open Society and Its Enemies

The heat is solid, like the crowd inside.
At a table under the awning
in front of the place, I go lizard
until the beautiful crazed waitress comes.
Iced tea and a bran muffin.
Dude on NPR
said we must learn to live without air-conditioning
and become more "versatile" creatures.
Yes, please, cream-cheese.

Across the way, at T. J. Maxx
and Filene's, my wife looks
for a blouse that at least looks like Neiman Marcus,
which if she fails is also here.
I visualize her judiciously-pursed
lips, which before the recession
graced Ann Taylor. There is a variable
of seven figures that equals a minimally
urbane life; it is known to the rich.

A disturbance in the restaurant ...
Those involved emerge. In the scrum
of shrieking does and bugling stags
and lawyers with drawn phones at ten paces,
I can't see: is it some
perve, from the johns, off his meds, impatient for service,
or one of those always surprising
eruptions of despair? And will it
delay my iced tea?

Then across the walkway, U.S. marshals
and obvious FBI
remove from one of the stores
someone else I can't see, who may have a beard
and melanin, or be one
of those corn-fed albinos who volunteer
to boil their brains Eastern-style instead
of in our native modes. He's praying
and/or shouting; I can't hear.

The feds are getting good at this.
But is my wife in that store? With
anthrax … ? Wildly I call.
She is trying on something that sounds sublime
and – grimly, triumphantly – cheap.
"Did you see anything?"
"Nothing we need." "Little excitement out here – "
(Actually it's over.) But she's
preoccupied, and asks for more time.

Although it's the same ten outlets
as anywhere, this mall tries
to make them look distinctive.
With holograms at each crossroad:
vast babies; athletes; the blue gods
from *Avatar;* approaching figures
that are the shoppers they approach, except
smiling; windows on the foam
of perilous seas in faery lands forlorn.

Only the giant CNN screen
may be a miscalculation –
a pod of whales in the oiled sea,
all dead or dying in agony,
appear a moment, not again.
The heat is stunning. I try to think,
but the only phrase that occurs is Olson's
"mu-sick" (from *Maximus),*
which all critics agree is tasteless.

And suddenly my bagel with cream cheese
and iced tea are there,
and are the platonic forms of themselves,
though the bagel has blueberries. From above,
the songs that soothe and inspire the crowd
have turned vocal. Sinatra "telling the story"
as someone said, Neil Young
sounding vulnerable, Janis cheerful,
the martyred Marley acclaiming wan love.

Quiet City

Beyond the cones of lamplight, the park
ruminates itself, the memory
of summer's lovers, and childhood
monsters fondly recreated
all night by passersby. In the theater district,
shows have let out, and audiences stand
silent a moment, unwilling
to relinquish images of one who may
or may not be the hero, like themselves.
Then buses come, and plazas empty
beneath loosening leaves, except
where café lights invite
unexpected necessary persons
to enter, briefly effecting
a deeper hush than that of loneliness.

Uptown, on a thousandth floor, behind infinite
drapery, a rich man reads
reports. It should be possible
secretly to open the secret valves
and rot the wiring, plumbing, bread
and lungs of those below; so that
he could walk out in his worst suit
and still be worshiped by the starving drowned.
He knows he's dreaming. In the dream
he's ashamed, and reconfigures
profits to benefit, without acclaim
for him, innumerable multitudes
starting tomorrow morning. Into which
he will only need to open his front door
and descend a single step.

Meanwhile his calculations float
like unheard music over unlocked houses
and tiny unlocked cars.
In sleep a million clerks and workers
turn to their wives and become satyrs
and centaurs, their wives nymphs,
their children hippogriffs and dragons
happy in feathers and claws, and the poor

spiders, coyotes, trickster-figures
of former cultures. And there are gods among them
or they are gods, and feast and toast
each other to justify
retroactively this heavy slumber.
Sated, the Minotaur renounces flesh;
even the envious Cerberus drinks and sleeps.

Temüjin Becomes Genghis

Yesterday he was made Khan.
A wind across the steppe attacks his words.
It doesn't matter. What matters is
he is seen – on a stallion, on a hill,
invoking ancestors
and raising the horsetail standard –
by sixty thousand warriors.
They are Naimans, Merkits, Tatars, Uighurs, Keraits, all
now Mongols. Have been made one,
and his, by marriage, oath, defeat,
betrayal and its punishment – the noble death
that spills no blood. They spend weeks
in the saddle. They can fire an arrow a second.
They pierce their horses' necks to drink.
They are always filthy.
When Temüjin now Genghis waves
his standard towards the west –
his motives include border security, fate,
contempt for life, and monopoly of the Silk Road –
they will raze Samarkand and Baghdad
to bones and dust, enslave Bulgars, Russians, Poles
and Chinese. But now comes a pause:
the Khan is having a vision.
He sees a palatial, covered bazaar,
unnaturally white. It is lit by hanging moons
and flashing colored serpents.
Its stalls, full of delicate clothes
and mysterious objects, are fronted
by acres of a thing he barely knows:
glass. His attention is drawn
to a kind of cart, lifted by magic
from floor to floor. A family of gods
steps from it, walking slowly among
the strange-featured crowd. The gods
are almost perfectly spherical.
Their faces bear the sleepy lack
of expression and the smile of bodhisattvas.
Absently they inspect the shops.
The Khan shares his tribe's attitude
towards religion – it's a private matter. But if

the easeful gods in the souk of Heaven wish
to bless his armies, he can only praise.
The meanest groom in the distance hears
his joyful shout, and sees
his standard lay its claim. Forward, my minions.

Conceit

These red-brick-white-trims
will scarcely have time
to ask why honest gypsum and
silicates were assigned
that form, before they escape it.
The lamppost and fireplug,
more focused, enjoy their gardens
of rust. Lawns and trees
are solid bourgeois, but dogs
resemble the efforts of
sophisticates trying to be simple:
embarrassing; sweet in places.
Only cars conceive a purpose,
but it's collective, not what you think.
"All is Mind," said the swami; that's
what happens to profundity.
When I'm dust, I'll resume
my interrupted conversation
with dust, and this time
reach a conclusion.

The Former Tenants

The town-house where the group home was
isn't selling. Perhaps it's the recession;
perhaps the barred windows, odd in this neighborhood.
Or an echo of screams in the walls.
Except that such effluvia don't exist.
Paint cures what it covers; people live
dreamlessly where prisons were, and torture.

Which probably didn't happen here.
The caregivers were mostly big and ponderous,
not patient so much as having
their disgust under control, accustomed to it.
They seemed, when outside, leading their charges
to the van for visits to specialists
or day-trips, like bison herding people.

Pale, nervous, stooped and hooting
people. People who stopped and cried
and had to be convinced to move.
A few, judged harmless and unlikely to be harmed,
ranged freely: the sunken-eyed and somehow
mouthless man who inched his way
to the corner. The youth

of forty who strode with an empty backpack,
shouting in whispers. The small
man-mountain. The earnestly,
shapelessly gabbling, crew-cut one,
visible only from certain
angles as a woman, who wanted to be friendly
but wanted above all a cigarette.

Gone now – mysteriously, but not really.
For years across the street I tried
to grasp what they saw, failed. Now only the bars
remain. And stained cheap walls
awaiting the revival of the market,
young upscale couples, children;
preserved meanwhile by a thin coat of pity.

Reception Theory

In the late work, we often see him
frantic to escape
the "sealed room." But when he opens
a door or window, he hesitates,
then closes it. Seldom writes
about love: it's where he
long since decided
to *live*, not think, not observe – at least,
not for public consumption.
As for "nature," his stance
resembles that of the old Jewess
in *Lacombe, Lucien*.
Improbably rescued from deportation,
tenuously safe
on a farm in the Midi, she is drawn,
one twilight, to a mysterious sound –
a cricket on a weed – and
bends to inspect it. It still pertains
to the goyim, the murderers
who claimed all space
for themselves; they can keep it.
He would rather invoke old movies.

Again and again in the late work,
spring leaves block
his view of a street. Should he use
"a street," with its general appeal,
or insist on "the Parkway across the river"
for its petty honesty?
The "perfect" day, before humidity,
bugs, and the sweat
of the inert, is as much
a function of physics
as the sewage drowning Nashville,
the dying Gulf, the minds
of the BP spokesman and the Times Square bomber.
We see him, looking rather vacant, make
this note. We see him
remembering Hawking saying, "I am free
in my mind." (Discuss.)

What he wants is evidently
the sort of *advocacy-*
as-criticism one finds
in Sartre's essays of the Forties.

The Man

Despite the risk, which is small
for the seldom photographed,
I treasure quasi-unprotected
passages from limo doors
to the doors of older buildings.
One day on such a sidewalk I'm approached
by a ragged malodorous fanatic
who, in the instant before he's blocked,
cries, *Jesus died for you.*
All afternoon, at meetings,
in the presence of lawyers
who smile as I sign things,
at the club, and at dinner,
thoughts of that encounter
return. That night
I gaze at the lights of the city below.
They extend in my mind
beyond the horizon to the towns
that huddle around wire fences
protecting kids from vacant factories.
I imagine the people,
some bravely not drinking
nor abusing each other in those towns,
and bless them in my heart; but am drawn
on by the lights to other places
where I have or sold an interest:
the little cities, with their touching new
museums of something-or-other,
austere parks, people gamely
still sending out resumes and standing in line.
Then the prairies, the box stores, the prisons, the farms …
In a kind of rapture, I see
the mountains and lingering day out there;
the deserts thirsty ambition crosses;
the incomparable
roads along which sleepless drivers,
skirting my former maquiladoras
(now themselves elegiac, outdated),
bestow on the heartland
their loads of methamphetamine. Everywhere

there is striving, everywhere people
I bless in my heart, as I think I've
already stated. Everyone dies for me.

The Bagpiper

-Derain, *Le Joueur de Cornemuse,* 1911

When for the first time
the townspeople heard music –
noises the stranger drew
from his unfamiliar object – they didn't halt,
only paused, didn't fall to their knees,
only glared. Yet they knew instantly
what it meant. It would complicate and crowd
perception, bend what had been
their straight line. Loud in a place
where only flood and fire disturbed,
it was sophisticated, putting them to shame
before imagined elsewheres.
The *doubleness* of each sound
the thing made mocked
their accent and their solemn narrowness.
Its endless drone belabored them
with the Ideal. There in the square
the townspeople laid hands
on the stranger, though not on his machine:
who knew what it might
infect with its last squeal?

Backlit in a large but peeling room,
a dyspeptic pyramid
combined the powers of money, state, and church.
When the mob had brought the piper
before it and left,
it rumbled, "We serve Time.
To serve means to adhere,
not alter or anticipate.
Our method is suppression of the senses.
To buy what is sold,
despising it and self,
yet with contempt becoming habit and,
like any habit, comfort.
To love what is given:
the sour breath of another
as familiar as one's own;
the stone wearing through centuries

of whitewash; the doubtful light.
By dawn you must be far away from here."

But at dawn the piper stood
on a ridge outside town. Some
perplexity had slowed him,
and petulance almost changed
his sketchy moody features.
Who was (he wondered) that fat silhouette?
The *Monsieur Bertin* of Ingres, the famous
"Buddha of the Bourgeoisie," by way
of Magritte's Keeper of Cardboard Keys and Chalice?
I know that the secret tunnel
to paradise runs
clockwise and counterclockwise
through the walls of the world's museums:
it's how I travel, how I happened here.
But tyranny has no passage there;
he had no right to bid me stay or go.
And what is this children's tale
of a town without music?
All cultures sing – at their rotting end,
they've little else. This isn't an early world,
nor I created to be Orpheus.
Unless … Here he pondered

the view. It was improved
by distance. The road
behind him forked, defined
a square around a pond
or inlet of the sea.
Pollarded trees, red roofs,
and everywhere the Golden Section –
it seemed the goal of travels. Yet he knew
how killer crowds erupt
from even well-posed lanes
and won't stop unless time is stopped.
A bird approached the birch,
expansive and knowing, beside him.
Both moved so wonderfully.
The piper primed his bag and gripped
the chanter, sighed that he must leave forever,
and put the mouthpiece to his lips and blew.

He Had Many Castles

This one was by a lake.
Mountains would have been nice, but
there was only the lake, and a forest
from which had come his bed, parquet, and gallows.
Beyond lay his villages and farms.

It was hot. We wandered back inside.
Portraits along the stairwell showed
the chin he married into, the nose he brought.
Again we admired silver, porcelain,
armor, tiles and other art,

reminding ourselves that memory
edits out discomfort
and boredom, injects richness.
Concentrate on colors, the graceful angles.
Fix them in your mind.

On our flight home, GM went bust;
the mortgage market started to unravel.
We became older, more crotchety,
and no longer able to travel.

In Case of Emergency

As far as the eye can see is farther
than it wants. The dying and reluctantly
living fill the courtyard, sidewalk, streets.
Rain tries to wash them,
but when it passes, blood again insists
it is the only color, the way a virus
attempts to make all life into itself.
We see selectively, for otherwise
there would be no inside
and outside, no room to move, the dead
no longer neatly wrapped and piled
for disposal, and we would join them.

Meanwhile, sleep has forgotten us,
the way distinctions forget
those who retain only a look,
a cough, and, at best, data for us,
tears for themselves and sometimes, still, each other.
They have us, of course, as we have them,
and the little, moment by moment, we can do.
One could say peace is achieved
in this noise, and justice in the midst
of basic crime. However,
to say that one would have to dream,
and dreams require sleep.

Yet on breaks, though there are none, in
a spare square yard of this place
that has none, behind a clean
and solid door, in nonexistent silence
and soft light whether from a lamp or sky,
we shape and furnish a room.
We build it together, each alone,
with sufficient compass for all
who struggle outside to stand,
exhausted as always but less,
and gaze, merely gaze at a space
that isn't an altar, with no lie on that altar.

CPSIA information can be obtained
at www.ICGtesting.com
Printed in the USA
FFOW05n1715230215

9 781632 750198